As a leader in this Golden Age of Transformation, Mariana is here to help human beings realise who they truly are.

Through the power of her presence, writings and spoken word, Mariana sets up a portal for you to quantum jump into the Fifth Dimension of Reality. Until you personally experience this quantum jump, no words can describe the feeling of Divinity and Wholeness of Being that awaits you.

You will love what a connection with Mariana can do for you. I highly recommend you taste and see for yourself!

Michelle Stanton

Mariana reminded me that it is ok to be vulnerable and sensitive … and to explore my gifts with even more effervescence than I had previously dared. Her book touches a forgotten part in our soul, sparks it with a loving hug and tells it not to be afraid.

Monika Mundell

Mariana's work is the embodiment of us; the whole. She expresses her wisdom through channels of the divine, on purpose and with mission. Trust her beautiful words to sweep you into the midst of a world you dream of; a world beyond fantasy and reality—a new paradigm. She takes us on a journey of mankind and the soul merged as one.

Mariana is a true messenger of the soul's expression; a wish you seek to fulfill; a yearning for deeper connections with the higher self. Read divine presence in every word of this book, and you will feel gateways unlock and portals activate within.

Mariana's work is truly of divine essence, and has something for everyone; whether you're looking for an afternoon pick me up, a rise and shine, high vibe 'come alive' prose, or an activation into a deeper understanding of your own magnificence. Mariana can inspire us all!

Lisa Bombardieri (heyLis.)

Mariana is a Visionary Messenger, Author and Speaker. Mariana's work is about Life and Truth. It is about reconnecting people to True Consciousness, True Connection and True Reality.

Life—The Dance of the Divine delights, inspires, activates and shifts readers to take quantum leaps in their lives through experiencing and understanding the book's powerful writings.

Mariana says she is not here to teach, for at a core level we already know Who We Are in Truth. Her work helps us remember who We Are and inspires us to step into our magnificent Truth. Each piece in *Life—The Dance of the Divine* carries beauty, poignancy and wisdom.

Experience what Mariana calls "Aha Moments" when you recognise Truth at a deep level, giving rise to Consciousness and the quantum leaps of Understanding, and Wisdom and Creativity that flows from it.

Mariana

LIFE—THE DANCE OF THE DIVINE

Published by Starseed Publishing
www.mariana.life

First published 2022

Copyright © Mariana, 2022

The moral right of the author has been asserted.

All rights reserved. Without limiting the rights under copyright restricted above, no part of this publication may be reproduced, stored in or introduced into a retrieval system, or transmitted, in any form or by any means (electronic, mechanical, photocopying, recording or otherwise), without the prior written permission of the copyright owner and publisher of this book.

 A catalogue record for this book is available from the National Library of Australia

ISBN 978 0 6456459 2 7 (POD pbk)

Cover painting by Carol J Argent
Designed and typeset by Blue Wren Books
Printed by Ingram Spark

I dedicate this book in Love, Honour and Gratitude To All
And to our Connection To All
As we travel on this magnificent Journey of Life through Creation

—*To All on this magnificent Blue-Green Jewel of a world we share*
—*To ALL in this Grand Universe that is our Home*
—*To The Divine, To Light, To Love and To ALL in realms seen and unseen in this Glorious Dance of Life*

The Dance of Life—The Dance of The Divine.

Contents

PART ONE

Our Story

Our Story   2

PART TWO

Dance the Dance of Life

A Blessing for All with the Eyes that See	9
A Divine Moment Recognized for the Divinity It Is	11
A Hum Pervades the Silence	13
A Moment that We have Birthed Together	15
A Moment When God Touches Creation and It Touches Him Back	17
A Moment when the World of Man Merges with the World of God	19
A Moment when We Dance with the Beauty of Life	20
All are Expressions of The Divine	23
All Is	24
An Iridescent Dance in the Heavens	28
And God Comes Out to Play on the Canvas of the Sky	31
And Life is Glorified	32
And the Sweet Symphony of Sound We Create Rises to the Heavens	34
Another Divine Day on Planet Earth	37
Be Still and Hear the Song of the Ocean	39
Come Come—Come Play	41
Come Dance the Dance of Life!!	42
Do You Not See that You Have Them Already?	45
Everywhere I look is the Work of Genius at Play	46

For It Is at the Boundaries We Feel Our Own Existence	49
Give Thanks for Your Beautiful Life on a Beautiful World in a Beautiful Body	50
Go Play with the Wind and Let it Take You on its Journeys	52
God Painting His Brushstrokes Across Infinity	55
How Loved I Am to Share in its Life	57
How Precious is my Little Cricket	59
I Sit Resisting the Power Around Me	61
I Smile as I go and Play with Creation	63
I Smile as I Sink Into the Silence	65
I Touched Creation and I Am Complete	66
I Touched Eternity and It Touched Me Back	68
Is This Not The Most Important Thing You Could Be Doing?	71
It Intoxicates All the Senses at Once	73
Join in the Wonderland of God's Creation	75
Life!! Life!! Glorious Life!!	77
My God How Beautiful!!	79
My Heart Joins in the Song and My Being Joins in the Dance	80
Oblivious to the Potential that Awaits	83
Our Ability to Touch The Truth of the Moment	83
Perhaps my Life is Not so Petty after All	85
Play in The Symphony of Life—You Are a Part of It	87
Remember Your Sense of Adventure?	89
Self Witnessing Self	90
So Beautiful my Eyes Can Scarcely Contain It	93
So Far from the Madding Crowd	94
Some of Our Grandest Achievements	97
Step out My Beautiful Ones to the Truth of your Home	98
Swimming Through This Glorious Moment	101
The Beauty of Your Experience Heralds The Beauty of Creation	103
The Choice of Whether We Choose it—Is Entirely Ours!!	104
The Dance of Life, The Dance of The Divine	106
The Delight of the Moment	109
The Ebb and Flow that Makes Life Possible	111
The Flow of The Day and The Flow of Life	112
The Inbreath and Outbreath of the Day	115

The Majesty of Life in Front of Your Eyes	117
The Moment When Man Touches Creation	119
The Radiance of the Light on a Full Moon Night	120
The Raw Power of The Dance of The Elements	123
The Silence Contains the Answers	124
The Song of the Sunset	127
They Open our Heart Amongst the Chaos	129
This Most Divine of Moments	131
This Most Precious Jewel in the Crown of God	133
This Tiny Patch of this Beautiful World as it Meanders on its Journey Through Time	134
To Fall in Love—Passionately, Deeply, Madly in Love—with Life!!	136
Tonight Belongs to the Stars	139
"Value it and Respect it for at a Core Level it is You"	140
Wake Up, Wake Up Sonnambula	143
We All on this Glorious Planet Are Children of the Sun	145
Were You There at the Dawn of this Glorious New Day?	146
What a Joy it is to Be Alive	149
What Does it All Mean Dearest Ones?	149
What if—Life is Life!!	151
Your Truth—Is Not in Your Doing—It is in Your Living	153

PART THREE

The Journey of Man

A Celebration of The Journey of Man	157
A Weekend of Expansion and My Soul Rejoices	158
Four Old Men on The Jetty	160
How Special it is to Be Alive	163
I Like Your Trees	164
It is New Year's Eve and There is Joy in the Air	166
Life Caressing Life	170
Life Flowing from Night to Day—Back to Night—Back to Day	173
My Heart Sings and My Soul Soars	175

The Masters Have Arrived	177
The Priorities of This Short and Extraordinary Life	179
Their Selfless Love has built Mountains and Bridges across Time and Space	181
We Are All Children of this Magnificent World	182
We Have Much to Celebrate and Much to Look Forward To	184
Who and What Will You Be in This Game of Life?	189

PART FOUR

The Journey of the Soul

A New Phase Begins	192
A Point of Connection Between God and Man	194
An Infinitesimal Probability—And Yet, We Are Here!!	197
And So It Flows—In Infinity, From Infinity	198
And So the Ripples Expand Across Creation	201
And There Will Be Much Celebration in the Heavens and on Earth	202
Are You Enjoying Our Dance?	204
As the Soul Walks from its Night to the Dawn	206
Bring Your Truth to this Beautiful Realm and Watch Miracles Happen	208
Connection to the Grand Universe Beyond	210
Hundredfold to the Power of Infinity	212
Is The Breeze Touching Me or Am I Touching the Breeze?	214
It Sings, We Sing—We Sing, It Sings	216
Keep Your Desires Alive	218
Know Your Truth	220
Let The Dance Begin	222
Life is a Destination	224
Life is Life and You are All One	226
My Words Expand Into the Night and Flow into Infinity	228
Nothing is Lost	230
Ourselves Calling us Home	232
Possibilities Yet To Become	235
Rest Gently Dearest Soul	236
Shine the Light of Your Sun for All to See	239

The Brushstrokes of a Grand Masterpiece	240
The Dance of Light with Density	242
The Dance of the Divine	244
The Gift of True Life	246
The Journey Of The Soul	248
The Moment Contains the All	251
True Choice	252
Truth of My Being	254
"Wake Up, Wake Up My Beautiful Children"	257
What a Grand Journey We Travel	258
Who and What will You BE On the Blank Canvass of Your Day?	263
You Are The Purpose	264

PART FIVE

The Driver is Love

The Driver is Love	268

PART ONE
....

Our Story

Our Story

I want to tell you a story—a story of Love and Life—a story of poverty and hardship, barons and peasants, family and laughter—a story of Dreams and Hopes—and above all, a story of Triumph

The story starts on a rocky mountain overlooking the plains below and the azure blue of the Ionian Sea in the distance and the glorious Mediterranean sky above
A small village called Placanica, perched precariously on a mountain top in Southern Italy
Its age goes back into time immemorial
Its fortifications of high walls and gates have witnessed much in its long history
If the walls could speak they would recount stories of invasion and conquests, victory and defeats throughout its history
About burning and pillaging, about rape and destruction—the land, the animals, the people
Of noble men and slaves—of feudal lords and serfs
About heartache and loss—and shattered dreams
And eking out an existence on its meagre soil
Of hunger and need

But somehow through all of this—the enduring spirit of those that came before me—to hold on at all costs—to move forward and better their lives for their children and their children and their children—for generations to come
How do I know? I who was not born there, nor have I ever lived there

I know because I stand on their shoulders in order to stand
on the mountain top
For their story is my story—and my story is their story

I did not meet my grandparents or those that came before them
But I did know my parents and I carry their legacy
They carried the pain and the sorrow and the dreams of all
that came before them
It was all for us—the children and our children and our children's
children—it was all for the future
I don't know if they ever understood this—but it was more
important to them than breathing—their every breath carried the
hope for the future generations
And I proudly stand here and say *"We have triumphed"*
And I humbly give them Gratitude for all they have endured and
all they have dared to dream—for it has come to fruition

They have travelled time and travelled the oceans and brought us
to the future
And gently placed us at its feet in this beautiful land of Australia

"We have done all we can do" I hear them whisper
*"We have unshackled you from the grip of hunger and poverty
and of subservience to those that would rule over you
You are free!!
It is up to you now"*

Cont …

And so the baton is handed over and my journey begins
My journey starts on the mountain tops—and it is for me to
launch it to the skies like an eagle taking to wing
And I will take them with me
They will now travel on my wings
And they will witness a future so Glorious—that they could not
have begun to imagine it all those years ago, in a small village
called Placanica perched precariously on a rocky mountain top
overlooking the azure blue of the Ionian Sea.

PART TWO

Dance the Dance of Life

A Blessing for All with the Eyes that See

The moon sits high in the night sky
Full in the glory of the Radiance of Our Sun
The Stars keep it company
The night is still
The glowing lights of the city shimmer in the water
The cars speed by on their journeys—movement in time
The Angels fly through the Heavens—their wings reflected
by the Light of the night
A Jewel in Time—forever remembered, forever treasured
The Brilliance defies words
The vibrant beauty surpasses all that man can create
I herald this Most Glorious Moment
A Blessing for All with the Eyes that See

*"Where are you Dear Ones that you should let this Most
Sacred Moment slip through your fingers?*
*Too busy caught in the smallness of your world to herald
the Wonder of the Heavens in the palm of your hands?*
If you only knew."

A Divine Moment Recognized for the Divinity It Is

The waterfall spectacular as it baubles down the rock face
The scene stunning beyond measure
The water pool below the waterfall spills over an embankment
The reeds slowly sway in the cool early morning air
The Sun rises above the hills in the background
The wanderer butterfly sits quietly amongst the grass near the pool—opening and shutting its wings as it picks up energy from the early morning Sun
The Sun feels delicious on my skin
Its Light and its Life and its warmth seep through the top of my head and seep through my body and seep through my Being
I breathe in the Life all around me and lose myself in the beat of the Moment—in the beat of Life—in the splendour of the Moment
All judgment suspended
All dissolves as I beat with the Dance of Life as it pulses around me —the rocks, the water, the grasses, the butterflies, the birds, the Sun
The power of Life
The power of the Moment
All is Divine—all is in Unison
All is Beautiful—all is Fulfilment—all is Special
A Divine Moment shared
A Divine Moment recognized for the Divinity It Is
A Sacred Moment—A Sacred Union
The Purpose of Life fulfilled
Stunning beyond description.

A Hum Pervades the Silence

The depth of the night—the Divine night
The Silence goes forever
How can I capture its Stillness?
How can I capture its Expanse?
How can I capture its Divinity?
How can I capture its Infinity?
It captivates me—it allures me—it intoxicates me
The velvety smoothness of the night
The piercing lights of man's world and God's Heaven
The breeze is still
The sounds are silent but for the distant drone of cars
on some far away road
The river is silent
Even the sound of crickets is muted
A Hum pervades the Silence
A sound that I have not heard before—never seeking it,
never expecting it
How Beautiful
Is it the sound of Mother Earth as she breathes?
Perhaps it is the Resonance of her Life
How interesting is the realization that it is always present
But it is only in the Silence that we hear it
The sound of Mother Earth
Like the heartbeat of a mother ever-present to a child as
it cuddles in her bosom—comforting and reassuring
How Beautiful She Is
She holds us close to her Heart and her heartbeat reassures
us—Mother is at Home
How Blessed We Are.

A Moment that We have Birthed Together

On a glorious earth morning I sit on the patio
Enjoying the Divinity of the Moment
Enjoying the Infinite blue sky above and the cool
crispness in the air
Enjoying the squawk of the seagulls as they stir from
their sleep
Enjoying the Sun—our Glorious Sun—as it casts its
Life Force so that all may live
The clouds glisten with its Light and the Earth thaws
with its warmth
My Heart sings the Song of the morning
As I Connect with the Earth and the Sun and the wind
and the clouds and the birds and all Life around me as
we travel on our journeys through time
A Moment etched Forever in the memories of all
that Connected
And we will look back to this Moment and smile for
that which we shared
A Moment that we have birthed together—in Beauty and
in Honour and in Reverence to the Glorious Life that
we are privileged to live and privileged to experience
A Moment of pure Creation on this most beautiful of worlds
What a glorious day this is.

A Moment When God Touches Creation and It Touches Him Back

The night is dark
The air is still
A balmy summer's evening—exquisite beyond description
The wind feels deliciously cool on my skin and plays with my hair
The Stars shimmer in the night sky
Across the way, a home proclaims the celebration of the coming Christmas with lights a rich deep blue and flashing red and green—colours so familiar with this festive season
The bridge glows a Divine blue in the darkness of the night
The night is sublime
I sit in the Stillness of the Moment and feel Life as it meanders on its journey through time
A Moment etched forever in the journey of my Life
A Moment etched forever in the Consciousness of this beautiful Moment
To be always remembered with Gratitude and Reverence
A Moment Exalted and Cherished
A Moment when God touches his creation and it touches him back

"What a Joy you are to behold My Beautiful Ones."

A Moment when the World of Man Merges with the World of God

Night has settled in at the end of a hot day
I sit on my Beloved Rocks overlooking my Beloved Ocean
The delicious cool breeze slowly wafts past
The pathway at the top of the rocks winds its way around
the shoreline
The scene stunning beyond description
I breathe deep and relax into the Beauty of the Moment
A Moment of Divine Perfection
Twinkling lights light up the night in all directions
—the lights of the boats out at sea—the night too beautiful
to come to shore
—the myriad lights of the city as it winds its way around the bay
All mimic the Lights of the Heavens that fill the night sky
At a distance the twinkling lights of the city could be the twinkling
lights of the boats which could be the twinkling Lights of the Heavens
A Moment when the world of Man Merges with the world of God
I smile—All is Well with the world, All is Well!!

A Moment when We Dance with the Beauty of Life

I sit on my Beloved Rocks overlooking the Ocean and the shore
The Sun has set and dusk settles in over the land
The vista is surreal, unreal
Surely it is part of a dream—Beautiful beyond measure
As I sit on my Beloved Rocks taking it all in—I feel like an
observer, an alien to the scene—seeing it for the first time and
watching Life in its detail as it rolls along
The jewels of the city lights, as they curve around the bay
The clouds, interspersed with the muted colours of the fading sunset,
as they spread to the horizon
The Sea, as it rolls to the shore—every wave announcing its Presence
with the sound of its familiar signature
The fisherman, as he patiently holds his line beyond the waves
The young dolphin, as it rises and falls in the water, looking for
a tasty meal near the rocks
The sea breeze, barely a whisper
The small fishing boats, speeding to shore in the fading light
The couple, walking their dog on the beach
A typical summer's evening at the end of a hot day
The smells, the activities, the colours—all merge to create the
living kaleidoscope below me
How curious, each piece is vital
The Moment would not be complete without the fisherman, or
the dolphin or the waves as they break on the shore—they are
an integral part of this Moment
It is as if the Moment is Whole unto itself—it is complete—
nothing can be added nor needs to be
It fills—fulfils all the senses and all the feelings and all the thoughts
Nothing can be criticized—for it is perfection

In order to experience this Moment—we need to suspend our judgement of it and allow ourselves to observe it
To sit quietly on top of the rocks and open ourselves to it
And to allow it to be what it is
And then watch Miracles happen—as it opens its Truth to us
And we are privileged to both witness and share a Moment stunning beyond description
A Moment when we Dance with the Beauty of Life around us
And in one Lifetime we are Blessed with Infinite Moments just like these
For it is not the scene in the Moment that defines its beauty
It is the Moment itself and our participation of it.

All are Expressions of The Divine

A long day and much to do in the world of manifested reality
At the end of the long day I sit on the top balcony and stare
at the Moon
How spectacular it looks bathing in the Light of our Sun and
surrounded by a halo of colours reflected through the luminous
white clouds
The night is calm and still
Barely a whisper of a breeze meanders by
I look across the balcony and watch the cars on the road in the
distance and watch a plane cross the landscape as it comes in
to land at the nearby airport
I breathe deep and let the frenetic day wash away in the Stillness
of the Moment
The Stars peek through the clouds
It is as if the night is holding me tight and holding me still—
and in that embrace my brain goes Silent
I smile and my Awareness heightens as the Joy of the experience
of this spectacular Moment becomes my world
I close my eyes as I dock in and Reconnect
—to the Centre of Stillness
—and to My Centre and My Truth
—and to the Centre of this Magnificent Reality I am a part of
For these Centres are the same
All are Expressions of The Divine.

All Is

What grandeur separates all that we are
And all that we do
What Moments in time determine our destiny
All is up for grabs
All is forgotten
All is remembered
Ah! The paradoxes of our existence
What does it all mean?

Separation of our destiny
Separation of our Being
Separation of our thinking
Separation of our grandest ideals
Separation of our Humanity
All is Divine
All Is—as it should Be
Humanity, destiny, separation—All Are One
All are meaningful
All rest in the bosom of the Divine
"Fret not Little Ones
For you are not forgotten."

The chorus of Angels sing of your Glory
You are Beautiful
You Are ... All that Is.

Your Joy fills the corners of the Universe
We smile
You laugh
We are One
Amen.

You must know your Humanity to know your Destiny
You must know your Destiny to know your Divinity
You must know your Divinity to know your Truth
Ah! All Is …

What—you weep in Joy or sorrow?
What—you laugh with wonder or excitement?
What—you sing in sadness or laughter?
Do you not see?
It is All the same
The tears, the Joy, the sorrow, the wonder, the thrill of just Being
One with Self—One with All—One with One.

My little cherub sits in the tree
And laughs as he watches the blossom bloom
What innocence, what thrill, what Joy
As I watch my little cherub sitting in the tree.

𝒞ont …

As the flower blooms so does Life
As the Sun rises above the horizon so does the Joy of the morning
How can one be without the other?
It cannot—for All Is Connected.

Sleep with Joy for the morning comes
Sing with laughter for evening sets
Ah! The cycle of the day
A Joy to behold
You are Blessed.

Sing the Song of the rainbow
For its melody fills the Joy of man.

Much is remembered—much is forgotten
All is well in the hearts of man
All is well.

Sing my little dove of the Joy of the dawn
Sing with the Song that bursts from your Heart
You Bless us All.

Your Truth Envelops Us
Your Song Delights Us
Your Joy Connects Us.

An Iridescent Dance in the Heavens

Another glorious day awakens on planet Earth
The air is still
As the birds wake from their slumber their soft warble rises
from the trees
The doves gently coo their song of Peace and Joy
The little swallow lifts its head and sings its glorious tune—
calling to the world
The seagulls stir and whisper their familiar squawk
The breeze drifts slowly by
The cool air carries the sounds of the dawn
The river pulses with Life—its ripples shimmer the colours
of the day as it comes alive
The sky magnificent as it heralds the dawn
An Iridescent Dance in the Heavens as God paints his Living
ever-changing Masterpiece
First deep blue with strokes of dazzling red flying off the hills
in the distance
The backdrop gradually lightens to azure in places, light blue
in some and but a hint of blue in others
The fluorescent reds and oranges and whites Dance across the
sky—a chameleon of Light
The Sun pierces over the horizon—a Sacred Moment in the day
The birds go silent—they understand the significance
The Brilliance of our Sun bathes the world with its Light and
bathes the world with its Life Force and has done so ever since
this Beautiful World came into existence

It lifts our eyes and lifts our Hearts and lifts our Souls and
Connects us all—to Life
The day is bathed in the gifts from our Sun as we all breathe in
its Life—the Earth, the shimmering water, the grass, the plants,
the birds, us—All Living Things
Then there is a Moment as the Sun rises—a pause in time—
as we stop and we acknowledge it for its Life and for its
Gift of Life
This most Beautiful Sun and its most Precious Child—this Jewel
of a World that we share
How Blessed we all are—to Share such Life.

And God Comes Out to Play on the Canvas of the Sky

The Sun prepares its descent on the horizon
And God comes out to play on the canvas of the sky
A three hundred and sixty degree living canvas
lights up the Heavens
As God masterfully creates with his palette of
colours and forms
Fluorescent whites—subtle pinks—fiery oranges—
burning reds and endless blues
The clouds ever-morphing into Infinite forms
—some streaking across the sky inviting us to ride them
to another adventure
—some fluffy and soft reminding us of a gentle caress
The colours and forms swirl and change and shift and
blend as God displays his Mastery
There for man to enjoy
On this most Divine Jewel of a World that we are
privileged to share.

And Life is Glorified

Exhausted I sit—missing the beauty of the night
Too tired to relish the coolness of the breeze on my face
And yet—in the pause something stirs
The crispness of the night caresses my face and the
velvety darkness wraps me in its embrace
My awareness rises as I sink beyond the shallowness
of my beliefs—into the Silence
The heightened sounds of the cars as they whirl in
the distance
The coolness of the breeze as it meanders over my hands
The plane as it rises overhead taking its precious cargo
to faraway lands
The richness of the night
The stillness
My heart skips a beat in the quiet thrill of the Moment
The beauty rises
—surpassing the illusion of the pettiness of our small lives
as they fade into the oblivion—insignificant to the
awesomeness of this Moment
The thrill rises within of the expanding Awareness
—of what is—Truth
—of what is—Real
As I humbly witness the power of Life around me
The Beat of the Moment
The sounds as they pulse through time
The lights as they pierce the coolness

My mind quietens—heightening—rising to meet it—
witnessing—as I merge with Reality—feeling its Truth
Privileged
Humbled
Blessed am I
Blessed are We
The Purpose fulfilled
We are One
And Life is Glorified.

And the Sweet Symphony of Sound We Create Rises to the Heavens

The cool breeze blows gently at this most Divine of hours
The time when the colours of the day take on an amber glow as our
Sun prepares its descent to end another Glorious Day on planet Earth
The birds sing their evening song with a subdued gentle bauble that
wafts from the trees
The temperature is a Divine twenty-five degrees Celsius—
Perfection on a perfect day
I sit under my beloved trees and do nothing
I am an observer, a witness, a participant of this special Moment
A Moment that co-exists with the world of Man and yet is not part
of it—like a separate reality always present but never intruding
There for those with the Eyes that See and the Mind that Knows and
the Heart that Loves and Appreciates
I watch the kaleidoscope of dancing shadows created by the play
of the wind through the trees
I watch the insects—silhouetted by the light—as they Dance over
the plants
I watch the plants as they sway in the gentle breeze
I delight in the sensation of the wind as it ebbs and flows over
my body
I tune in to the myriad of birds as they gently sing their song
I sit silently and join in this Living Symphony that I am sharing
at this Divine time of the day

I Do Nothing and yet I Have All
For I am Dancing the Song of the Sunset with all around me
My Heart sways and I Sing my Song
Its melody joins in with all Life around me at this special time on this most Precious World
And the sweet Symphony of Sound we Create gently wafts on the breeze and rises to the Heavens
And the Angels smile and Join In.

Another Divine Day on Planet Earth

The Silence before the dawn
It pervades the air as the night slowly fades and the day slowly awakens
All is still as the world stirs from its slumber
My little cricket is fast asleep after a night of staying sentinel outside my window
Even in sleep I delight at its Presence
The birds slowly stir in the trees and softly, softly begin their song
Their Gift to the day
All is in readiness—the world stirs but it awaits the Moment
The wind slowly meanders over the water—as if in a holding pattern
I too wait in anticipation for the Moment
An Eternity passes—and then in one Glorious Moment
Our Sun bursts over the hills
Its rays pierce the remnants of the night that instantly dissolve in its Presence
The giver of Life on our beautiful world has arrived
I breathe in its gift as my body rises to greet it and thank it for allowing me to share in another glorious day
Its Light warms my face and warms my Heart and warms my Soul
The day begins anew—another Divine day on planet Earth
I am ready and like a child I look forward in anticipation to this Gift of another day
I wonder what great adventures today will bring?

Be Still and Hear the Song of the Ocean

The Sea—the Divine Sea
My eyes can barely contain it
The blue—the Divine Blue
How we take it for granted
Do you not know its Power?
Do you not know its Love?
Do you not know its Divinity?
It courses through your veins
It is the Mother of your Life
And you see it not—you feel it not
It sings its Song to you and you hear it not

"Hush, Dear Ones, hush the chaos of your lives
Be still and hear the Song of the Ocean
The Song it has sung to you since you came into
Being
Do you remember the Lullaby it sang as you came
to this beautiful world?
Do you remember your Delight the first time you
splashed in its waves and you heard its Song?
You knew it then
Hush—Be Still—hear its Song for you
It is the vessel of your Life
Hear it
Its Song for you is Now
It Drifts on the Wind—It Falls with the Rain
—It Rolls with the Waves
Delight in its Beauty—Share in its Splendour
It is Yours
You are Blessed."

Come Come—Come Play

The Dance of Life, the Divine Dance
How awesome it is as I join in high above the Ocean
sitting on the rocks
The wind, the Divine wind caresses my face and teases
my skirt and laughs through my hair
It teases me as it envelopes my body

"Come come—come play
Come come—come with me I'll carry you with me
Come and join in as we roll over the Ocean, as we roll
over the world
Come come—come experience the world through my
Essence
Come come—come feel me as I Dance over the world
and Dance in the heavens
Come come—come laugh as we set the world in motion
Come come—come feel me
And the delight you feel in feeling me—is the delight in
feeling yourself through me
And the delight I feel—is the delight of feeling myself
through you"

And so the ripples expand across creation
—the Dance of Creation, the Dance of Life
Life touching Life
Love touching Love
Self touching Self
Creation experiencing the Divine
The Divine experiencing Creation

"You are much Loved My Dearest Ones."

Come Dance the Dance of Life!!

The sunset stretches as far as the eyes can see
Setting the Ocean on fire with the fiery colours of its Being
As above below
The breeze refreshes the body, the mind and the Soul after a stifling hot day
Breathe it in—breathe in the beauty—breathe in the Life
Glorious beyond description

"Do you not see Dearest Ones I have laid this out for you?
The best of creation for my Beloved Children
And yet you walk past my gift for you and lose yourself in the constructed world of man
Mistaken identity—misplaced attention
You are too busy lost in the tools of your world—and do not hear the Truth of your Heart—and the Truth of your Spirit—and the Truth of your Soul
You cloister yourselves indoors—hypnotized by a screen
The illusion within the illusion
You cherish buildings and material things over your fellow man
You believe the pretence of your limitation—over your Unbounded Truth
You become lost in the boundaries of your mind
How sad

Open your Eyes Dearest—and open your Heart—to the Glorious Creation that is Your Home
Respect it and value it
And you will witness Miracles unfold before your Eyes
As Creation opens its Truth to you

So Come Dearest Ones
Venture beyond the limitations you believe to be real and
Come Dance the Dance of Life!!
That is there waiting for you
—in every breath—in every Moment
And watch your illusionary boundaries dissolve
as you touch Eternity."

Do You Not See that You Have Them Already?

The start of the Divine day as the Sun pierces the horizon
The Joy and Thrill of Life
To feel Life all around me and within me as it courses through my veins
To feel the Joy and Love of Life
To feel the Happiness of Life
To feel the Splendour and Wonder of Life
To feel the Passion and Thrill of Life
To feel the Intelligence of Life
To feel the Tenderness and Compassion of Life
To feel the Peace and Tranquillity of Life
To feel the Excitement of Life
To feel the Wisdom and Power of Life
To feel the Abundance and Prosperity of Life
To feel the Dance and Rhythm of Life

"Why do you seek these Dearest Ones?
Do you not see that you have them already?
They are yours to enjoy—in every Divine breath—in every Divine Moment—of every Divine day of your existence
So you can experience Life
So You can experience You
For You are Life and You are all these things as is all Life"

The Dance and Rhythm of Life—the Wonder of it All.

Everywhere I look is the Work of Genius at Play

The Sun is setting—its Divine colours glow red, orange and yellow and streak across the sky
The wind is up and the sea rises and falls to its command
The waves, white caps as they roll to shore
A black-shouldered kite hovers high in the sky over the sand dunes searching for an evening meal
How Glorious is the bird against the backdrop of a fiery sky
It elegantly and expertly hovers over the land keeping its body stationary and rapidly beating its wings
What an Extraordinary sight
I marvel at the Genius that created it
Way above the capacity of man
And I marvel at the creative Genius all around me
The Glorious Ocean—Alive with Life
The brilliant sky with clouds that glow with the colours of the sunset
The wind—the Glorious Wind
My Beloved Rocks—each unique
I realize that everything around me is the Creation of Genius
The man as he walks his dogs
The dogs as they play along the beach
The clouds now turn to a crimson red—a rare sight
How Spectacular it is
And how Spectacular is my body to have the ability to see it and interpret it

And how Fantastic are the waves as they break on the shore
And how Fantastic is my body to hear the waves as they break on the shore
And how Fabulous is the wind as it twirls around my body
And how Fabulous is my body to be able to feel the wind as it twirls around it
Everywhere I look in this Glorious Wonderland is the work of Genius at play
How Blessed we are to have the opportunity to experience it.

For It Is at the Boundaries We Feel Our Own Existence

The Sun is up—the bridge is down
The traffic is gone—taking its chaos with it
Another Glorious Day unfolds
The Silence—the Sun—the breeze—and the laughter
of children!!
It's school holidays—"*Yippee!!*"
And the children have reclaimed the street
The young boys dressed in their cool outfits tear down
the slopes off the rise—impressing each other with their
fancy moves
One Moment laughing—one Moment yelping
What a Joy it is
They could just as easily be skiing off a tall mountain
—or base jumping—or diving—or dancing
It is the same
They push their boundaries and feel the Excitement
—the Thrill—the Exhilaration—the Pulse—of Life!!
For it is at the boundaries we feel our own existence
Our relentless pursuit—to push the boundaries
To reach the Moment where time stands still
And in that Precious Moment
To experience both our mortality and Divinity together
How Blessed we are.

Give Thanks for Your Beautiful Life on a Beautiful World in a Beautiful Body

The days roll on
No rhyme, no reason given—it just happens
And in that happening lies the complacency

"Imagine if you had to make the day unfold in order to survive?
What a different life you would have
But it is not so
The day has been Created for you in all its Glorious Splendour
The Brilliance of the morning air and the sunrise and the breeze and the chirp of the birds
It is all there for you for when you wake from your slumber
Do you comprehend the Depth of Love that Created such a Beautiful World?
Imagine if you had to make each breath in order to survive?
What a different life you would have
But it is not so
Your beautiful bodies have been Created for you in all their Splendour
The power of the breath, the beat of the heart, the glory of emotions and the complexity of your beautiful brains
Do you comprehend the Depth of Love that Created such a Beautiful Being?
So wake up each day My Beautiful Ones and give thanks for your Beautiful Life on a Beautiful World in a Beautiful Body

And then go and Enjoy your existence
Savour each Moment
Savour each experience
Value each breath
And Go Dance My Beautiful Ones—Go Dance with Life
You are much Blessed and you are much Loved My Dearest Ones—Enjoy."

Go Play with the Wind and Let it Take You on its Journeys

Life in motion
The Wind flies over the Ocean
White caps as far as the eyes can see under the power of the Wind
The clouds scurry along under the power of the skies
The Rain comes and the rain goes
It sweeps clean the stagnation of summer and the stagnation in our body and the stagnation in our lives
It breathes new Life into all Life

"Go feel the Wind—breathe it in
Feel it course through your veins
Feel it reach into the depth of Your Being and blow away the stagnation in Your Life—stagnation of thoughts and actions—stagnation dulling your beauty and awareness
Feel it breathe new beginnings into your world
And put a spring in your step
As you start your Life anew—in this Moment—Now
Go outside Dearest Ones and join in with Life
It beats through your Being
Go Play with the Wind and let it take you on its journeys
Go surf the waves of the Ocean as they tumble to the shore
Go speed glide with the birds as they play on the thermals
Go Dearest and open your Heart and open your Vision
And go Play with Life

Go Dance—Dance the Dance of Life
And the more you join in, the more you will feel it course through Your Being
Renewing every aspect of who You Are
Until you are Full
Full with the beauty and richness that is Life
Full with the beauty and richness that is You
And then My Dearest, you will know what it means to be Truly Alive and not just live."

God Painting His Brushstrokes Across Infinity

The sky lights up—Magnificent beyond the clumsy description we give it
The clouds, alive and ever-changing—now fluorescing yellow—streak across the sky from the hills across the heavens to the Sea
God is at play—masterfully Creating his Divine canvas
The birds have eased their song as the dawn awakens
Even they are in awe of the Splendour around them
On this glorious morning the canvas of the sky captivates the Moment
The river is still and joins in with the Dance in the heavens—alive with the changing colours of the sky
God is at Home—playing in the heavens—mastery beyond imagining
Brush in hand, skilfully he strokes his brush across the sky and sets in motion a kaleidoscope of ever-changing colours
The pure Genius of Creation
Perhaps that is how Creation started
God painting his brushstrokes across Infinity and then delighting in its ever-changing landscape.

How Loved I Am to Share in its Life

The full moon shines through the cool night
The Brilliance of the Light it reflects from our Sun
is spectacular beyond words
As I share in its beauty
Breathing it in
Soaking it through all the pores of my Being
Nourishing my body—my mind—and my Soul
As I bathe in it, all the petty thoughts and concerns
dissolve away in the power of the Light
How Loved am I to share in its Glory—to share in
its Life
Glory be to God in the Highest
On Earth as it is in Heaven
Amen.

How Precious is my Little Cricket

The sun has set
The sky—hues of muted blues and greys and indigo
The clouds barely hints of white—a reminder of their
earlier brilliance
The stars are dreamily awakening
The breeze has eased so as not to disturb the arrival of
the night
Hark!!—the sound of my one little cricket in my sliver of
a garden bed filled with flowers
A smile beams across my Heart as I await in Silence for
its next call
How Delightful it is—the sound of my little cricket heralding
the night and keeping the Silence company
Perhaps it knows as it quietly chirps through the night that
it keeps me company as I sleep
How Precious is my little cricket.

I Sit Resisting the Power Around Me

I sit resisting the power around me
What foolishness!!
I release the stupidity
And join in the Song of Life
As it Dances around me
What Joy!!
Fulfilment at last.

I Smile as I go and Play with Creation

The day moves slowly as I sit having breakfast on my
patio—relishing each sip of espresso
I feel the breeze on my face and hear the coo of the doves
The world slips by and then the world slips away—far away
into the distance somewhere
The Silence seeps in
How curious—I realize the Silence is always there
Underneath the noise and chaos of our lives
How reassuring it is
To know of its Ever-Presence
Comforting to know that the Moment I get tired of the
confusion surrounding the Oh-so-important! trivia of
my Life
That I can go Home
And the road Home is the Silence
And as I dive deep into the Ocean of My World I smile as
I go and play with Creation
I Am Home.

I Smile as I Sink Into the Silence

It is early morning after a night of rain
The Rain, the Rain, the Glorious Rain
Much appreciated in the depth of summer
It is before dawn and man sleeps
The air is still and the inky darkness of the night is rich and full
Silence fills the Moment
Even the beautiful sound of crickets—singing their song in appreciation of the wet earth—does not disturb the Silence
I sit on the second-story balcony of my home
My beautiful home that my parents built oh so long ago
I look across the dark oval to the hills in the distance—the same hills and the same lights I enjoyed in the past from my patio overlooking the river
I look at the Stars in the heavens and smile at their familiar ever-presence
Time moves incessantly on in our world and there is comfort in the Stars which—compared to our short lives—appear Eternal
Their apparent constancy is comforting in our hectic twenty-first century existence and in a world of accelerating change
The coolness and the inky darkness on this Divine early morning feels Delicious
I breathe deep and Smile as I sink into the Silence
I Am contented and I Am Free.

I Touched Creation and I Am Complete

The Sun is inching its way towards the horizon getting
ready to end another Glorious Day
I go for a swim in my Beloved Ocean
The water is crisp and cool
Every cell in my Being breathes a sigh of delight
I have come Home—for the Ocean is Home for me
The tide is high and the waves lap against the rocks
Each wave moving to shore meets the surge returning
How wonderful
The Ocean is alive and I ride its in-breath and its out-breath
I lie on my back contented—Silent—for I have All I need and
All I Desire in this Moment
The waves carry me with them—how Delicious—how Special
as I move with their rhythm
I look up at the sky—a most spectacular vivid blue—its colour
is etched in my Soul
Ah!! the Angels are out to play—taking up the vista and playing
hide and seek through the clouds
The translucent white of their Presence fills the sky—some large
and distinct—some mere wisps
I often see this spectacular display at this time before the Sun
makes its journey over the horizon
It is as if the Angels come to share this most Sacred Moment—
when the Sun sits on the horizon and a gateway opens to the
world beyond
Perhaps they are an important part of this Precious Time at the
end of another Glorious Day on our world

Perhaps they come to remind us of who we are
Perhaps I see them because in this Moment I Am who I Am
Whatever the reason—whatever the purpose
I then I lie on the rocks with the waves gently lapping against them
I listen to the mesmerizing sound of the waves as they break
on the shore
I look to the horizon and watch our Glorious Sun touch the Ocean
And in this Moment I Am Fulfilled
And even if I did not share another Moment on this
Beautiful World
I could leave knowing that this journey was worthwhile
For this One Moment in time when I Am who I Am
And I have touched Creation
And I Am Complete.

I Touched Eternity and It Touched Me Back

Venus—spectacular Venus—and magnificent Jupiter have come to herald the dawn
On this cold deliciously crisp morning
Flanked by their sentinel of a lonely star, only they light up the sky
How magnificent—the brightest lights in the heavens on this glorious Earth day are two of our sibling planets come to greet us
They pierce the still dark sky with their Brilliance
The scene is stunning beyond words
As the dawn slowly rises a hint of muted orange brushes across the horizon
The river glows in the faint morning light
Just enough to light up the way of the canoeists as they silently glide past
The bridge in the distance glows a stunning cobalt blue—proclaiming the beauty that man can create
I sit on a bench on the riverbank—the pines my sentinels behind me
The day slowly stirs
Cyclists glide by in the dim light on the road behind the pines
The plane rises to the heavens on its journey with its precious cargo
The clouds slowly meander across the sky
The birds begin to chirp their songs in the trees
And so another Glorious Earth day begins anew

I rise from the seat and bow in Gratitude to the planets that
have come to greet us on this cold Earth morning
And I bow in Gratitude to the treasure of the Magnificent
Creation around me and that I am privileged to share
And as I turn my head to the day—people to see and things
to do—I smile as I leave the riverbank
For in these Precious Moments on this Beautiful Earth
morning—
I touched Eternity and it touched me back.

Is This Not The Most Important Thing You Could Be Doing?

The full moon seduces the night
I have an unease—that I should be doing something—
something more important!!
What folly!!
For as I Connect with this Moment
I experience Life in its Totality
I experience Truth in its Fullness and
I experience Joy in the Richness and Magnificence
of this Moment

"Dear Ones is this not the most important thing you could be doing?"

It Intoxicates All the Senses at Once

The stunning beauty of the night
Beautiful beyond imagining
Stunning beyond words
How do I embrace it all?
The full moon
The stillness of the night
The clouds streak across the sky luminescing with the light from the moon
The lights of the city pierce the crispness
The Stars twinkle with their familiar signature
Even Jupiter has graced us with its Presence
The water—a mirror—reflects back the beauty of the heavens
How do I do this Moment justice?
The beauty so overwhelming it intoxicates all the senses at once
Pure Divinity
How Blessed We Are.

Join in the Wonderland of God's Creation

I sit high on the rocks overlooking the sand and the Ocean
A panorama that stretches Forever
My Beloved Rocks—each one different—each one a personality
of different colours and different shapes and different feels as
they glow in the Presence of the Sun
The Ocean Dances with sunlight as far as the eyes can see
I sit contented and Free
The fresh wind whips over the Ocean and shears up the rocks
dancing with my skirt and laughing as it goes
It bellows under my skirt as if trying to lift me off

"Come, come" it whirls around me
"Come play—come join in the fun—come join in the game
We'll fly over the Ocean, surf the waves and play with the dolphins
You'll feel me play with your hair and Dance with your body
We'll rise up and up and glide with the albatross
We'll meet with the Angels as they fly with the clouds and Dance
across the sky
We'll watch the sailing boats below as they skim the waves
to the shore
And we'll Laugh with Delight as we Join in the Wonderland of
God's Creation."

Life!! Life!! Glorious Life!!

Life!! Life!! Glorious Life!!
Lest we forget as we lose ourselves in the Oh so trivial decisions and divisions of our daily lives

"Look up Dearest Ones—look to the skies and Remember
Who You Are and where you came from
Look to the Sun and give it Gratitude for Life
Look to the Ocean and go play with the Dolphins
Roll in the iridescent green of new grass and feel Mother Earth caressing you
When you lose yourself in getting through the day
Pull yourself back to Your Truth and re-centre to the purpose of Life
Your adventure on your beautiful world will end Dearest Ones in but the blink of an eye—this you cannot change
So do not waste your Precious Gift of time lost in the trivia of unimportant emotions
This is Your Life—this is Your Adventure
Value each Precious Breath
Value each Precious Moment
Look to the Heavens and Remember Who You Are
And then my Dearest Ones Dance!!—Dance the Dance of Life!!
And in these Precious Moments
God and Creation meet and pirouette through Time to Eternity."

My God How Beautiful!!

The liquid night deep in its richness
The moon hangs in the night sky
How awesome it looks reflecting the splendour
of the Light of our Sun
Our Sun that Lights up the darkness
The lights of man pierce the crisp air—stirring a memory
The ripples on the water shimmer in the reflection of
the moon
The sounds—a hum in the distance
How small I feel and how awkward I am in my clumsy
expression of a Moment that is glorious beyond the words
that are yet to be invented and beyond my limited capacity
to express it
And Yet!
I Am here witnessing it—sharing it
Perhaps—this is as it should Be
A Moment of Pure Connection
Lovemaking at its most profound
As we pierce Eternity
We are Complete
My God how Beautiful!!

My Heart Joins in the Song and My Being Joins in the Dance

I sit on the top balcony of my beautiful home
It is early morning and the cool wind is Delicious—an
interlude in the heat of summer
I look to the hills in the distance
A thick cloud hangs across the horizon and shrouds them
in darkness—a contrast to the ever-brightening glow of the
dawning day
A lone light hangs in the sky in the east—a shiny beacon
It is not a star but Venus—our sister planet—keeping vigil
on this most Divine of mornings
The tall majestic gums rustle gently in the breeze
I hear the gentle song of the birds as they begin to awaken
It wafts from the trees and greets the day in all directions
—true surround sound
I take a deep breath and allow the peace of this Precious
Time of day fill my Being
The chaos of the frenetic pace of our modern human urban
existence is but a dream in this Moment
I Connect to the ever-changing kaleidoscope
of Life around me
—the brightening iridescent colours of the sky
—the ever-richer sound of the birds as they awaken
—and the delicious coolness of the breeze as it eddies
over my skin

My mind is still—quietly it sits—Silent and alert
Delighting in the experience of the fullness and
richness of Life as it Dances around me
My Heart joins in the Song and my Being joins in the
Dance of Life
In this Precious Moment on this Divine Journey on this
Most Beautiful of Worlds.

Oblivious to the Potential that Awaits

The crispness of the night—delicious
Its haunting beauty—seduces all the senses
The Silence—overwhelming
Man oblivious to the Potential that awaits
He sits indoors—a prisoner to a false reality
What sadness that he should miss this Moment.

Our Ability to Touch The Truth of the Moment

The night is still
The darkness is rich and full in its depth
The stars sheepishly hide behind the clouds
The cars journey on their way across the river
The Moment is Full
It is not the busy-ness of our lives that decides our fulfilment
But our ability to touch The Truth of the Moment
And our journey is complete
We have come Home.

Perhaps my Life is Not so Petty after All

The Rain pelts down obscuring the vista
The Wind howls over the Ocean onto the land
The Sea a mass of frothing waves
The Clouds tear across the sky
Clouds grey and heavy with their cargo interspersed with
patches of Glorious blue sky
Today belongs to the Elements
As I sit and watch in awe as they play around me
A witness to a scene far greater than my petty little life
And yet I do Witness it
And I do Feel it
And I do Acknowledge it
Perhaps my Life is not so petty after all
As I smile and bow in Honour to the Grandeur around me.

Play in The Symphony of Life—
You Are a Part of It

The day is alive
The Wind—the Rain—the Sun—the Sea
All join in a Symphony of movement and sound—
touch and experience
Effortlessly they roll from one to the other
Playing in the Heavens
Oblivious to the power they wield
Delighting Man and God alike
All join in this game of Life
Even the Angels are seen flying across the sky
playing hide and seek with the clouds and tumbling
with the Wind
Be still—and join in the Grandeur
Fly with the Wind
Roll with the waves
Dance with the Rain
Shine with the Sun
Play in the Symphony of Life
You are part of it.

Remember Your Sense of Adventure?

The glory of the night
The heartbeat of the Moment
All is remembered
All is forgotten

"Don't take it all so seriously Little Ones
Enjoy the playground of Life I have laid out for you
You will come home soon enough
Enjoy the journey
Enjoy the ride
It is meant to be an adventure
Remember your Curiosity as a child?
Remember your Love of discovery?
Remember your sense of Adventure?
Remember who you are My Dearest Ones
How could it be anything other than perfect
You are much Loved."

Self Witnessing Self

The night, the glorious night
All is still—and yet—Life stirs around me
The night is filled with Stars shining dimly in the distance
The moon shines brightly tonight
I sit on the riverbank—the tall pines my sentinels behind me
The river stretches in front of me
It glistens as the ripples light up from the lights across the way
and from the Glorious Light of our Sun reflecting off the moon
The murmur of the ripples as they gently caress the riverbank
is mesmerizing
The new bridge in the distance lights up with the colours of the rainbow—one after the other
Now a spectacular cobalt blue—a jewel against the velvety darkness of the night
I watch as three blobs of white come meandering down the middle of the river
Ah!—it is three pelicans floating by
How surreal they look

"Going for an evening stroll down the river are we?
Oh may I join you dear friends? Haha!"

The cool breeze flows through my hair and gently caresses my face
I stretch my gaze to the Heavens—past the smallness of my human reality—and melt into the glory around me

My senses heighten
—I see it all at once—I feel it all at once
—the bridge, the trees, the water, the breeze, the inkiness
of the night, the white clouds, the moon, Ah! Mars—
our brother planet watching over us—and the beautiful Stars
of our Milky Way
The smallness of my human reality disappears into the
Silence and dissolves into the Moment
I become part of all around me
The Separation dissolves and yet the individuality still exists
How curious I feel both
—the seer and the seen
—the one witnessing and the witnessed
—the observer and the observed
Man witnessing Creation—Creation witnessing Man
Life witnessing Life—Self witnessing Self
The Dance of the Divine.

So Beautiful my Eyes Can Scarcely Contain It

The Sun, the Sun, the Glorious Sun
Warming up the frosty winter morning
The drive through the hills Divine
The hills glow with the green of new grass
The Divine colours of this Glorious World
Beautiful beyond words
I am speechless at the stunning scene rolling in front of me
So Beautiful my eyes can scarcely contain it
The haunting beauty of the iridescent green rolling hills
And the spectacular eucalypt trees rising from the land
—each tree unique with branches rising in all directions
An impressionist canvas on the face of the land
The air is still icy from the cool night but the body warms with the rising Sun

"What have we done to deserve such Magnificence?"

"Enjoy my Dearest Ones
 Enjoy the Wonderland of Creation that you are a part of
 Value it and Love it and it will Open its Truth to you
 And you will share treasures beyond your imaginings."

So Far from the Madding Crowd

A hectic day in a different city
A major metropolis in the world of Man
—heavy traffic, congestion, noise, appointments, phone calls, meetings
Argh! no street directory in the hire car!!
And the car's navigation system is taking me to my appointment via Pluto!!
All I needed to do was cut across the suburbs—a trip of around thirty minutes
An hour later it has led me into the heart of the mayhem of the city and down a dead-end alley way and staring at the river
How hilarious—there is a cosmic joke in here somewhere!
I finally get to my appointment—late!
My next scheduled meeting requires me to cross the city and drive out country
Apart from now running way behind schedule—I don't trust the navigation system
I don't particularly want to get there via Andromeda—although come to think of it, Andromeda could be fun!!
I cancel the meeting and I have a local give me the shortest route to the airport—literally on the back of an envelope
—Man One, Technology Zero!!
I am now hours early!!
On the way to the airport a flash of green in the distance captures my attention
Yes!!—a park—a green oasis
I find my way there down a shady side street
This diamond hidden in the bowels of man's concrete world

There is a plaque at one corner acknowledging the family that donated the park
I thank them for the generosity of their gift that I am now enjoying
It is stunning
It is not a manicured park but a natural oasis
The land rises and falls
There are the makings of a creek although all that remains is a stagnant pond—how sad
Regardless—the trees are tall and magnificent
The grass is lush and green and unkempt with weeds and leaves and twigs
I lie on the grass and close my eyes and let Nature bring me back to myself
I feel the wind caress my face and hear it rustle through the trees
The sunlight and shade play with my body
The grass feels soft and the earth feels deliciously cool
I breathe deep and smile
I have come Home—in this little oasis surrounded by the world of man and yet so far from the madding crowd
I lie here for an Eternity and renew my Being
As I get up I watch a wanderer butterfly as it plays over the grass— the stunning green grass
As I walk the wind picks up and billows under my skirt—so familiar on my Beloved Rocks next to my Beloved Ocean—as if greeting me in recognition of who I Am
I bow and I smile as I leave this Jewel of a hidden world
And I give it thanks for the Treasure it has given me and the Connection we have shared

"Thank You, Beautiful One, Thank You."

Some of Our Grandest Achievements

The clouds ablaze with colour
The waves meander to the shore—alive—beating with life
The Sun resplendent as it sinks towards the horizon
The clouds sweep across the sky—each one brushed with
the colours of its uniqueness
A Moment of pure Divinity
The time that man can touch the Sun
And walk through a Gateway to a world beyond
The golden hues streak across the Ocean and Dance on
the ripples
There is more gold in this Moment than man could crave
in a thousand lifetimes
The cormorants skim the waves—heads turned to Home
The Sun resplendent as it turns red—ready to end another
day on this most Divine of worlds
I sit humbly in the awesome power of the Sunset

*"Could it be to have the Awareness to connect to the Grandeur
of Life
And to have the Eyes that see and say 'YES—I See You!!'
And the Heart that feels and says 'YES—I Love You!!'
Are some of our Grandest Achievements?"*

Step out My Beautiful Ones to the Truth of your Home

It is Sunday and another spectacular day on planet Earth
The Sun is up, the wind is down and the earth is warming up after a frosty night
I sit on the steps next to the weir built across the river
Across the way is the airport and I watch the giant beasts lift into the air
Mortal man once believed it was beyond the realms of possibility to do so—and yet they now do and we accept it as a commonplace reality
Is the stretch so great to a Greater Reality?
I sit on the steps next to the weir and listen to the babbling water as it flows over and watch the wading birds as they walk the edge
The grass is a spectacular iridescent green interspersed with the subtle shades of the weeds amongst them—it all looks so perfect
What is it about the green of the plants that lifts our spirits?
The air is yet cool and the vast expanse of grass shines with droplets of dew—like a field of diamonds glistening in the Sun

"If you yearn for diamonds Dearest Ones—step out in the early morn and see the dew drops glistening on the plants
And if you yearn for gold—go to the Ocean at sunset and watch the Ocean glisten liquid gold as far as the eyes can see
And if you yearn for Freedom Dearest Ones—as you sit cloistered in some tiny room in some tiny corner of a man-made structure—then go outside and cast your eyes to the spectacular heavens that stretch forever—so vast your human brain cannot contain it

This is Your Home Dearest Ones—the expanse of the creation that you are privileged to be a part of and privileged to have the capacity to know it
Your pain of lack of that which you believe you do not have—is merely the self-imposed exile of the illusion of the lack within the game you play
And when you tire of the limitation of the game—step out My Beautiful Ones to the Truth of Your Home
—Expanses that stretch to Infinity
—Treasures beyond your capacity to contain
—And the Joy of the True Freedom that You Are
A Freedom that within the illusion you cannot even imagine
The choice is yours My Beautiful Ones."

Swimming Through This Glorious Moment

It is early morn
The Sun has risen and bathes the land with its Light
I sit in the backyard of my beautiful home after a restless night
The morning air is crisp and cool
A slight breeze meanders by
The morning sits in the Silence
—a Silence that pervades the air and pervades the Moment
I relish the Stillness
How Divine this Moment is
A peace and an alertness soaks through my Being as I tune in
—to the Silence
And to the morning Sun
And to the vivid green of the grass
And to the stunning beauty of the blossoms on the trees
And to the gentle chirping of the birds as they sing their songs of the morning
It is as if I am swimming through this Glorious Moment
Rolling effortlessly through the richness that this Moment is
The Silence
The atmosphere thick with life-sustaining oxygen
The Sun as it streams its life-force to us
The sway of Life as it flourishes in this extraordinary richness
What a Special Moment
And what a Special Place
And what a Special Privilege it is
To experience this Extraordinary Life we live.

The Beauty of Your Experience Heralds The Beauty of Creation

A perfect day on planet Earth
It is midday
I sit on my Beloved Rocks rising above my Beloved Ocean—
their colours fluoresce in the Sun
The temperature—a spectacular twenty degrees Celsius
The breeze—cool and delicious as it billows up my body
The sky—a perfect azure blue—gleams in the dazzling white Radiance of our Sun overhead
The clouds—white, fluffy and inviting as they travel on their journey to other shores
The Sea—a perfect blue-green with brilliant white caps—as it flows to shore and greets the land
The Sea calls to me to join in the experience
The sailing boats—white blips against the horizon
The father and daughter on the shore—the simplicity of their meandering along the edge picking up shells
The couples with their dogs playing in the distance
What a Perfect Moment on a Perfect Day

"The Joy of the Moment Dearest Ones is always Perfect
Enjoy the Beauty of your experience for it heralds The Beauty of Creation
Do you understand
—that you could not experience beauty if you were not Beauty
—that you could not experience perfection if you were not Perfection?
The Delight of Self experiencing Self
How Perfect."

The Choice of Whether We Choose it—
Is Entirely Ours!!

I sit at the edge of the tiny harbour—man-made for the small fishing boats
I sit at the edge of the water—tucked amongst the rocks—tucked away from the world
How Spectacular the rocks are—so individual
—the Magnificent colours of greys and oranges and fiery reds and whites and auburns
—all tell the story of their beginnings forged in the annuals of time—long, long ago when the Earth was young
And so I sit on the Magnificent Rocks looking out to the tiny harbour sheltered from the wind
The water moves and proclaims its own Life as it gently laps to the shore
The sound of each wave as it greets the shore is mesmerizing
—as if sharing its story at the end of a long adventure
A dolphin pops to the surface, takes a breath and magically disappears in this tiny harbour sheltered from the wind
The shore is blanketed with seaweed which mutes the sounds of the world around
All that can be heard is the constant whoosh of the Ocean in the distance as it greets the shore and moves in and out to a hidden rhythm
—perhaps it is the Ocean breathing
A little band of swallows dart over the seaweed at high speed—how skilled they are

I wonder what they seek?
—maybe some morsel of food on the wing
—or maybe just playing—speed flying over the rises and falls of the seaweed
The sky is magnificent in its hues of blue—deep and rich overhead fading to a hint of barely blue on the horizon
The Sun Resplendent as ever Lights up the world and all that share it
The clouds varied and Magnificent as the Angels play in the Heavens
I wouldn't miss this for anything

"So remember—when the Oh so important trivia! of your daily lives seems to consume your world
And your brains are overloaded with the incessant bombardment of the horrific travesties that are thrust on our fellow man and our fellow co-travellers and our beautiful world
Stop! and go find a piece of Heaven away from the madding crowd
For it also exists—Here and Now
And in Every Moment—of Every Day
And remember—that the Power of our Privileged and Magnificent Existence on this Jewel of a World is that
The Choice of Whether we Choose it Is Entirely Ours!!"

The Dance of Life, The Dance of The Divine

Alas! This is the last morning that the bridge is down
And then the chaos of Man will return to the street and swamp the Silence
I am filled with sadness and yet I stand here in Celebration and Gratitude for the gift I was given
As the bridge went down—the Silence without, connected to my Silence within
That Glorious Moment when the Realization came
—that the Silence of the night—is My Silence
—that the Brilliance of the Sun—is My Brilliance
—that the Dance of the wind—is My Dance
—that the Pulse of Life around me—is the Pulse of Life Within Me
—that the Glorious Treasure of this Magnificent World—is the Glorious Treasure of My Being
That Life is Life and All Is One
That as I Honour the Life around me—I Honour my Life and all Life
And God delights in his own Truth
My Gratitude runs deep for this Precious Time I shared with the Beauty around me in the Silence when the bridge was down
The bridge will return and yet the Treasure of that time will continue for it is anchored in my Being
And I will carry it with me on my continuing journeys on this Beautiful World and Beyond
For it is etched in the Now beyond Time

And if ever I wish to return to those Precious Times I spent
—dancing down the centre of the road
—or making love to the night
—or melting at the Light reflecting off the full moon
—or marvelling at the chirp of the birds as they awaken to another glorious day
—or hearing the wind flow over the river
—or melting at the rising dawn
—or delighting in the Sun as it bursts over the horizon
I can go within and access these Precious Moments in the Eternal Now
Or I can look around me wherever I am, whatever I am doing and smile
For the Pulse of Life I experienced in those Precious Moments is the same Pulse of Life that beats through my Being
And in every Moment
And in every Space
And in Everything
Now and throughout time and beyond
And this treasure is
Man experiencing Life
Life experiencing Life
And God experiencing God through his creation
And I humbly give thanks to share in this Glorious Dance
The Dance of Life, the Dance of the Divine.

The Delight of the Moment

The Delight of the Moment

"Why do you will more Dear Ones?
  Do you not see that the Moment contains the All?
  How can you will more than the All?
  The lack is not in the Moment but in your realization of the Moment
  Gain the realization and you will understand that the Universe
  lies at your feet
  And then your Life will be fulfilled
  For you have All—in every breath—in every blink—in every Moment
  Of every day of your Life here on this beautiful world and beyond."

The Ebb and Flow that Makes Life Possible

The Wind howls across the Ocean
The Ocean a sea of frothing waves under the command
of the skies
White caps as far as the eyes can see
Clouds scurry across the vista playing hide and seek
with the morning Sun
The seagulls speed glide to their destination
—Wee!!!!! Whoops!!—as they put their Life on the line
The Wind—the master of the day—shows off its talent
Its power ebbs and surges at will
Its movement brings Life to this special world
Without it stagnation and decay
It skilfully decides the power of its force
A bringer of Life and order and a bringer of chaos
and destruction
The ebb and flow that makes Life possible
How awesome is this world.

The Flow of The Day and The Flow of Life

The Sun is setting over the Ocean
The breeze meanders by
A perfect day on planet Earth
My spirits lift and soar at the Divine Beauty of the Moment
Clouds streak across the sky
The Sun takes centre stage as it moves on its journey to end
another glorious day
As it descends to the horizon, the clouds change from grey
to white and then fluoresce with the spectacular yellows,
oranges and reds of our Sun
I sit on my Beloved Rocks and witness the Glory around me
The restaurant of the sailing club overlooking the Ocean
is bustling with activity
The children however are outdoors as if they intuitively know
the Splendour of the Moment
The young gangly teenage boys climb the rocks and discuss
'big boys' talk as they hop from one rock to the other—
a show of young macho virility
The younger boys speed skate down the incline of the bridge
to the boat ramp—how skilful they are—and then sit on their
skates in a circle talking the important talk of their age
What a delight it is to witness their games
The still younger children play in the sand—squealing as
they jump in and out of the shallow hole they have dug—how
sweet she looks, the child in her pretty pink skirt

A friend of theirs excitedly shouts as she runs towards them
—*"Ice cream is on the table!!"*
They send out a final squeal of delight and off they scurry—
with far more important things on their mind than playing
—Ice cream!!
The flow of the day and the flow of Life
What a Joy It Is
The Simplicity of it All
The Magnificence of it All
And how Blessed we are to share it.

The Inbreath and Outbreath of the Day

It is midday on a Sunday—on a Glorious autumn day
The earth is damp from the rain of the previous day
I sit in the backyard overlooking the lawns of the
school oval
There is a Stillness and a Silence in the air
A hint of a gentle breeze wafts by
The Sun is shining and creating dappled patterns
through the fluffy white clouds
There are no sounds from the human world
The only sounds are the muffled murmurs of birds—
cockatoos foraging on the lawns and others having subdued
conversations in the trees
The day is in a holding pattern
Life is taking a siesta in this little enclave of urban existence
A butterfly meanders by
The Stillness is Delicious
There is nothing to do
For this Moment is not about doing
It is about Stillness
Even time has slowed down
How curious—the inbreath and outbreath of the day.

The Majesty of Life in Front of Your Eyes

A Moment of Divine Beauty
A Moment of Divine Power
A Moment of Divine Revelation
The Sun awesome in its power as it sinks towards the horizon—words insignificant to the Splendour of its Presence
The Wind Majestic as it flows over the Ocean whipping up an orchestra of sound and motion
The Ocean Stunning as far as the eyes can see—
a ballet of movement dancing on its surface
Life in Motion
The Ocean stretches to the Infinity of the Sun as it sits on the horizon
The Sun a beacon to a world beyond

"Do you See Dearest Ones
The Majesty of Life in front of your eyes?"

The Moment When Man Touches Creation

The day is silent but for an occasional truck speeding
to or from the bridge under construction
The air is still
I sit here in the Silence having breakfast
My emotions are Still
My thoughts are Still
I travel the depths of the Silence
The food tastes Exquisite—the coffee Divine
The doves coo in the trees—the sound Delicious
One comes to drink at the bird bath I have left for them
How beautiful the dove is
In the chaos of our lives—we do—but we do not live
In the Silence—we Live—and we do
The experience of even one of these Precious Moments
makes the journey to this beautiful world worthwhile
The Moment when Man touches Creation

"What would your Life Be if it was filled with Infinite such experiences?"

The Radiance of the Light on a Full Moon Night

The full moon shines brightly tonight in the Splendour of the
Light of our Sun
A bright beacon in the night sky lighting the way on a
Divine night
How many generations of our ancestors have looked up to
the night sky and given thanks for that light
How many generations have, like me, enjoyed the beauty
of the Light on a full moon night
And their Hearts were lifted and their Souls sang—songs of Love
and songs of Joy
It is the end of a hot summer's day
The breeze has started to blow now and the stifling heat of the
day begins to dissipate
I sit on the top balcony enjoying the Peace of the Moment
The darkness of the night luminesces with the Light
How curious both the rich darkness of the night and the
Brilliance of the Light coexist—both are present adding to the
magic of this night
I am bathed in the smooth rich Radiance of the Light at this
Divine time of night and melt into its Presence
I breathe deep and move into the Silence
And as I do my Awareness of the Magnificence of where I Am
and the Life pulsing around me Heightens
I feel the brush of the breeze on my skin and I hear the rustle
of the leaves on the trees

I Merge into the Beauty of the Magnificence of the Expanse
of our Beautiful Home—as I sit on Mother Earth and stare
into the Infinite darkness of deep space
I Merge with the Silence and travel its path back Home
The Silence runs deep
I Smile
I Am Home
I Am Blessed.

The Raw Power of The Dance of The Elements

The night is dark
The night belongs to the Elements
They rule supreme tonight
The thunder rumbles ominously in the distance—heralding
their arrival
And then in a Moment they proclaim their Presence
And unleash their power as the thunder smashes overhead
and the lightning shatters the darkness
The Raw Elements of God have arrived
The Elemental Forces of Nature that make Life possible on this most
Precious of Worlds
They command—and in a flash the lights of man are extinguished
They will have no rivals
The world of Man goes dark and the world of Man goes silent
And then the Rain comes—pouring from the Heavens
How Special is this Moment
To witness the raw power of the Dance of the Elements

"Join in, join in Dearest Ones
—in the spectacular play of Creation in front of your eyes
Join in, join in Dearest Ones
—in the awesome power of the Elements as they ride across the skies."

The Silence Contains the Answers

A window in time
A gap in the hustle and bustle of modern man
The bridge is down
The traffic has ceased but for a local or lost one
A Gift
I walk the night—the Silence my companion
Deep runs our Connection
The noise of engines silent
No longer shattering the peace
I am consumed by the Beauty of the Moment
As I walk the river the Silence caresses me
The breeze dances on my face
The ripples on the river hum in the Silence
The lights—a kaleidoscope of Light
The Gift runs deep
And yet only I walk the night
The road is empty
I Dance along the middle—as a child grasping a
Moment that will soon disappear forever
My fellow man so engrossed in the noise of their lives
Too numbed by its hypnotic drone to hear—the Silence!
The Silence that will take them Home
The Home they crave
But they do not understand

They fill their lives with noise trying to fill the emptiness
And yet the Silence contains the answers

"Where are You My Dear Ones?
Your Gift awaits
Join me
For it holds that which you seek
This Gift shall go soon enough"

In Silence it awaits
I accept

"Thank you."

The Song of the Sunset

I sit under the Divine trees at my family home
It is sunset
The earth is damp after a day of Rain—Glorious Rain
After months of parched earth and summer heat
A sense of contentment pervades the air
And the plants, the animals and the earth all breathe easier
The Rain brings Life to our parched bodies and minds and souls
I listen to the birds at this most special time of day
There is an added sweetness in their song as if to say—

"All is well with the world"

I look between the Glorious trees at my home and watch the Sun
as it filters through the trees in the distance
—a dappled living kaleidoscope of colour
The Brilliance of the yellow sunset and the fluorescent clouds and
the Richness of the green leaves and the subtle browns of the trunks
of the trees
The tall majestic gums light up—fiery with the colours of the Sunset
Their branches Dance with the gentle breeze—in contrast to the tall
rigid pines behind them
I join in the Sacredness of this Moment
—relishing in the Song of the Sunset
A snapshot in the Symphony of Life
Its harmonies Divine—and melodies beautiful beyond description
This Beautiful Moment is etched forever in my memory of this Grand
Life I am privileged to Live and share with the Life around me
Glory be to God in the Highest—and in the world of Man.

They Open our Heart Amongst the Chaos

The cool morning air feels delicious on my skin
The day is still
I sit having breakfast on the patio in the shade of my
Beloved Tree where my doves live
They coo contentedly—unafraid of my Presence
They know I am a friend
What is it about the Presence of doves and their sound
that is so Powerful?
It stirs my Heart and stirs my Soul
Perhaps they are a Gift from Heaven
And come to Herald the road Home
They open our Hearts amongst the chaos
And in that opening—we can feel the Pulse of Life
that beats within us and through us and around us
The youngest of the doves sits on a high branch
and looks down at me
How beautiful it looks, perched amongst the greenery

"Thank you Little Ones—Thank You."

This Most Divine of Moments

I sit on a bench on the riverbank
The Sun is setting
And the homes across the river light up and shine with
the yellow and orange hues of our Sun—accentuated
by the contrast of the vivid green of the palm trees and
the lawns along the riverbank
The day is Glorious
A slight cool breeze tingles on my skin as it glides past
The laughter of children as they play on the opposite
bank of the river wafts across the water
A Perfect Day and a Perfect Moment
To Stop—and Enjoy!
And give Gratitude for this Most Divine of Moments
What a Joy it is to Be Alive.

This Most Precious Jewel in the Crown of God

The spectacular night envelopes me in its wonder
The full Moon shines brightly
The velvety night
The cool breeze
The water lit by moonlight
The clumsy words of man cannot describe the Beauty of the Moment
The clouds streak across the Heavens from the horizon—fanning out overhead from one point above the hills
They are beautiful beyond measure
Perhaps they are the Wings of the Angels streaming across the sky—enjoying this spectacular night with us on our most Glorious World
My eyes rise to greet them
I smile at the thought that the Heavens have come to play with us on our most Precious Home
On this most Precious Jewel in this wondrous Universe that we live in
This our most beautiful Home where the colours are dazzling and shimmering and iridescent
—the brilliant whites
—the vivid yellows and oranges and reds
—the stunning pinks and violets
—and the thousand shades of the magnificent greens and spectacular blues
If I were an Angel—I too would come and join in this most wondrous Wonderland of Creation
This most Precious Jewel in the Crown of God

"Welcome Dearest Angels, welcome to our Beautiful Home
  We are Privileged at your Presence."

This Tiny Patch of this Beautiful World as it Meanders on its Journey Through Time

I sit on the rocks overlooking the quaint harbour for the small fishing boats
It is sunset—at the end of a day made in Heaven
The fiery colours of the sunset streak across the Heavens
—stunning beyond measure
In this tiny quaint harbour—the tide is up and piles of seaweed languish in the water with nowhere to go
How odd—they look so beautiful in the fading light that glows golden on the water
As the light fades—the lights of the city and the lights of the heavens begin to merge seamlessly
As they glow ever-brighter they light up the way of the night
My Beloved Ocean moves with a million ripples and captures the fading light of the remnants of the day and the remnants of the sunset
The little fishing boats tear into the harbour as the light fades
—as if to say *"Oops should not have waited for that last fish!!"*
The last remnant of the sunset now stretches across the horizon—
a sliver of fiery iridescent red and orange and pink
What Genius thought up such spectacular colours?
I sit here contented beyond pleasure
In this Moment there is nothing I would rather be doing
—for nothing else exists than this Here and this Now
I am sharing this Precious Moment with this most Precious Place on this most Precious World
The Silence is broken with another small fishing boat scurrying to the boat ramp
How surreal it looks with its little red and green lights

This little harbour is often visited by dolphins—lately a mother and her precious little one
I have sat here many a sunset and watched her fish with her baby by her side
The baby dolphin mimics all her moves
The baby hasn't yet mastered breathing like its mother and sticks its whole head out of the water with every breath—
how Divine it looks!!
I marvel at the sight of them fishing—mother teaching baby
I hold my breath as they dive and stay underwater—for oh so, so long!—the baby can't possibly have such big lungs!!
I breathe a sigh of relief when I see the baby dolphin's little head popping out of the water for a breath
I laugh as I realize that I am mimicking their breathing and I am sure I am the one struggling the most!!
The night has now settled in and the stars take command of the sky
My eyes are drawn to the brightest of them
Ah! it is not a star at all but Venus, the evening star, as it graces our world—how special
I listen to the distant sound of the waves breaking on the shore
And watch a plane coming in low to land at the nearby airport
I sit and watch and join in with this tiny patch of this Beautiful World as it meanders on its journey through time
From one Precious Moment to the next Precious Moment
I wouldn't miss this for anything
How Blessed I Am.

To Fall in Love—Passionately, Deeply, Madly in Love—With Life!!

The night is silent
Man sleeps
There is no sound from man's world
How still is the Moment
The world belongs to the elements
The light reflecting from the full moon lights up the night and bathes the world in gentle light
The Stars resplendent as they pierce the night sky
The luminescent clouds scurry on their mission to another destination
The cool wind rustles through the trees along the river—the sound delicious to the senses
How interesting—man sleeps and the world goes on with Life of its own
The Stars do not ask our permission to shine
The clouds oblivious to man's existence
The wind untouched by man's presence
How strange—we go on with our chaotic lives—too busy to value the True Treasure of our Conscious Ability
In our misguided ignorance we think we can rule the world
In the naive simplicity of our misplaced self-importance—we think and act as if we have the power to rule over creation
Our universe is ageless with galaxies in their trillions or more and the number of stars infinite?
Our Sun is well over three billion years old
We live Oh! 70–120 years!
How can we possibly think we could make good rulers?
It would be laughable
If it wasn't so sad to comprehend the depth of the travesty of our ways

And witness the destruction and the suffering we are reeking in our wake—on this beautiful Jewel of a planet and all those that share it
God does not need us to rule over creation—God has that handled!
We have the Gift of Conscious Intelligence
—To comprehend the Magnificence of the Creation we share
—To Delight in it
—And to Dance with it
God can then witness Creation through the Delight of Man
How Glorious
—To look at the Sun and melt in its Presence
—To look at the Stars and marvel at the glory of the universe we share
—To play with the clouds and scurry with them to their next destination
—To feel the wind on our body and breathe in its Life as it rustles through the trees
—To dive to the depth of Silence and all that embraces
—To witness Life around us with all our senses
And breathe it in, intoxicating us to the tips of our Being
And to fall in love—passionately, deeply, madly in Love—With Life!!
To experience it—to swim in it—and Dance with it through every breathe—in every Moment
And share in the Magnificence of it all—Life and Creation—in all its Diversity— in all its Beauty—in all its Grandeur—and all its Splendour
And know that God shares in our Delight
And then as we end our short lives on this beautiful world
To leave with a smile on our face
And give thanks for a Glorious Life well lived.

Tonight Belongs to the Stars

The Silence pervades the night
The cool air wafts by—not wanting to disturb the peace
The darkness of the night intoxicating
Tonight belongs to the Stars
How strange it seems—that in the Silence the Stars
appear brighter
They dominate the night
A canopy of Brilliance above
As they beam their Presence into space
Coded messages of Light letting us know who they are
And Jupiter standing proud in the night sky
A voice for the planets amongst the stars
How Beautiful is our Home.

"Value it and Respect it for at a Core Level it is You"

The Peace—the Divine Peace—as I sit next to the waterfall nestled
amongst the hills that rise sharply on either side
It is before dawn and the ground and the air are cool and damp
The mesmerizing sound of the waterfall as it cascades to the pool
below captivates the Moment
How Delicious
How Precious—on a day normally filled with the sounds of a city—
with the incessant sound of traffic
Where would we be if the cars make no sound when they are driven?
Perhaps we could hear the birds sing
And where would we be if we respect Nature and our Connection
to it more than our man-made world?
It is not about not appreciating the wonderful advances that we have
made and are benefiting from
It is about considering what world could we be living in and enjoying
if we grant Nature and our Connection to it the importance that it
is to our Life and our wellbeing
How would Life improve if we give it the Respect and True Value that
Life and our Connection to Life—All Life—on this planet deserves
—human, our co-travellers the animals, the plants and Mother
Earth herself
On this most Special of Worlds
Ah! the Sun is rising over the hills—its Light and its warmth is
delicious on this cold frosty morning
I can feel the Life around me breathing in its Vitality

And the sound of the waterfall goes on
The Beautiful sound of moving Life as it tumbles on its way
What a Precious Moment—on a Precious World

"Value it, Dear Ones and Respect it
—this Precious Jewel of a World—for it nurtures your Life
Value it and Respect it
—for what you do to the world around you—you do to Yourself
Value it and Respect it—for it is part of All that You Are
Value it and Respect it—for at a Core Level it is You."

Wake Up, Wake Up Sonnambula

The Wind, the Wind, the Divine Wind—it Dances with Life
The Sun has risen over the horizon
Its Brilliance warms the wet earth
The air is Silent but for the wind that has taken centre stage
It pirouettes around the trees
bringing them to Life as they hum their song
It rolls over the water and the waves Dance to its tune
It is in control now
The seagulls speed through the air tumbling as they go
It caresses my face with its cool intoxicating freshness saying

"Wake up—wake up Sonnambula
Do not tarry
Join in—join in—in another Glorious Day on planet Earth
Do not miss a Moment—it is too Precious
There is time enough to sleep"

It teases me as it plays with my hair

"Come join me" it laughs
"I'll carry you with me and show you wonders you can only imagine
We'll fly through the heavens and Dance with the clouds
We'll roll over the Ocean and marvel at the wonders below
We'll Dance through the fields and shake the trees to Life
We will set the Symphony of Life in motion
resonating to the power of My Being
And we will share in the Delight of God's Creation."

We All on this Glorious Planet Are Children of the Sun

The Sun pierces the dawn as it rises above the hills
The clouds iridescent in the mantle of the Sun
The cool air wafts past—intoxicating as it touches my skin
The birds sing the arrival of the Light
The seagulls squawk in their numbers across the way
The river receives the Sun and reflects it back—a homage to its Beauty
I sit in Silence sharing in its Majesty
There for all its children
For we all on this glorious planet are Children of the Sun
Born of the death of its forebears and born of its Life
I give Homage and I give Gratitude for Life
Life I Am privileged to have and
Life I Am privileged to witness and share

"Where are you Dear Ones?
Awake from your slumber and share in the Glory of Life that awaits you
Open your eyes
It is but a Blink away."

Were You There at the Dawn of this Glorious New Day?

The cool morning air greets me as I go outside to share in the rise of a glorious morning
Most people and animals yet sleep
The Silence of the morning is intoxicating
The high clouds cover the sky—but for the gap between the hills and the clouds
The clouds glow an ever-brighter yellow as they take on the colours of the rising dawn
—in the ever-changing kaleidoscope of Life as it travels on its journey
I hear the first chirp of the birds as they rise from their sleep
What is it about the chirping of the birds that is so Beautiful?
The river flows on—with a thousand ripples moving on its surface
The trees gently flutter in the cool early breeze
The colours of the sky ever-changing
What words do I use to describe the scene—stunning maybe?
But how can words describe the scene?
For it is beyond sight—and beyond sound—and beyond feel
I Connect with it—and drink it with every pore of my Being
And in the Connection I Am Home
—Home to the Truth that is the scene
—and Home to the Truth that I Am
The clouds dominate the vista as their colours intensify and fluoresce a brilliant orange-red

"My God how Beautiful"

The sky lights up—now fluorescing yellow
The Dawn of a New Day greets the world

And then in a Moment the brilliant colours of the clouds fade
and disappear
A pause—as if the morning holds its breath
My eyes are drawn to the gap between the hills and the clouds
which glows an ever-brighter white yellow
And then there is the Moment—an Exquisite Moment—when the Sun
bursts over the hills
It fills the gap with its Radiance
The morning glows with its Essence as Life breathes in its Life Force
And then too soon the Sun disappears into the clouds—and all that
remains is an afterglow
At the same time drops of rain begin to fill the day

"Were you there Dear Ones?
Were you there at the Dawn of this Glorious New Day?
Or did you miss it and wake up to grey clouds and rain?
How Sad."

What a Joy it is to Be Alive

The Sweetness of the Morning
The Song of the Day
The Joy of the Light
The Richness of the cool Earth
Life as it moves and plays with All around me
What a Joy it is to be Alive.

What Does it All Mean Dearest Ones?

The Moment Divine beyond beauty
The Moment Beautiful beyond Divinity
The Moment Full unto itself
The Moment Empty awaiting the potential that is yet to exist
The Moment Divine beyond Divinity

"What does it all mean Dearest Ones?
What does it all mean?"

What if—Life is Life!!

The rain has come—the Glorious Rain
The Essence of Life, the food of the Soul
The night is dark but for the clouds that fluoresce against the grey sky
The flashes of lightning split the night
Like children we count and delight when we hear the familiar rumbling of the thunder
—as if we have shared in its making
The rain picks up force—loud it beats as it falls
A Gift from the heavens
How Delicious it is
Feel the Pulse of Life as it rises to drink the nectar from the heavens
In this Glorious Moment
As all Life Dances in Delight to the Rain
—it is the Connection of Life that we feel
What if we are not so different—people—animals—plants—and nature?
What If—Life is Life!!
And it is not a difference of Life that we see around us
—but a sliver of difference in expression?
For the Rain feeds us all—does it not?
And what if the Rain is also Life?
Life meeting Life—the Dance of Creation

"Open your eyes Dearest Ones
And see the treasure of the Dance of All Life around you
And Delight in its Connection."

Your Truth—Is Not in Your Doing—
It is in Your Living

The days go by—busy in the bustle of minutiae
What a travesty that we should miss the point of Being here in the first place
A piece of paper is never more important than the message that it carries
So why should the tedious mundane things we do possibly be more important than our ability to see the Splendour of this Glorious World
To taste the Divine freshness of reality around us
To smell the Richness we are a part of
To hear the baubles of Life as it bubbles along
To touch the Power of Life as it rises and falls

"Open your Hearts Dearest Ones
And open your Minds
And open your Love to the Truth of your existence
And each Moment will be delicious no matter what you do
For your Truth—is not in your doing—it is in your Living
We Love you Now and Always."

PART THREE

The Journey of Man

A Celebration of The Journey of Man

The Sun is shining on a Glorious Day
It is Sunday and the promenade of the new marina complex
is alive with people enjoying the restaurants, the cafés,
the boats—or just strolling along the promenade
The place to be—modern and fresh—trendy and chic
The Sun glistens on the million-dollar boats moored in
the marina
The people laugh and chat
Amidst the wealthy ambience of their surroundings they
enjoy time away from the routine and stresses of their lives
Their spirits lift
I sit at a restaurant—alfresco—overlooking the shimmering
water and the gleaming boats
I smile as I watch a daughter and her elderly parents at the
next table
They are enjoying a meal and this Moment together
—surrounded by the excitement and bustle of others also
sharing an interlude in their daily lives
The modern apartments surrounding the marina glow in
the midday Sun
In this little enclave of modern urban human society
A Celebration of the Journey of Man.

A Weekend of Expansion and My Soul Rejoices

I sit on the majestic roots of a Moreton Bay fig in a small
lush park—a green oasis on a rise above the centre of a
large metropolis
The rich earth beneath my feet is cool and damp
It is early morning and the coolness of the previous night
lingers in the air
I breathe in the moist, cool fresh air—it feels so delicious
to my lungs
Such a Divine interlude—during a weekend cloistered
in a modern hotel near the city square
A hotel where I swim in a small artificial pool—and I breathe
recycled air and sit all day in a large room with artificial lights
and no windows
So far away from my Beloved Ocean where I fly and run and
swim free
And yet it is a weekend of expansion and my Soul rejoices
As I sit in the small park high above the centre of the city I
look across the vista
The majestic tower of the City Hall glows in the early
morning light and takes centre stage amongst the skyscrapers
towering behind it
A medley of old and new—lest we forget where we came from
and where we are going
It is Sunday and the hustle and bustle and life in the city
square on the Friday night has fallen silent
The bronze lions—so lovingly caressed that night—now keep
lonely vigil on this cool Sunday morning

How majestic they look—shining in the morning Sun
The time has come that I must return to the large hotel with its artificial lights and recycled air
And I give thanks for this interlude I spent sitting on the roots of the majestic fig tree in this oasis near the city centre
And I give thanks for the Beautiful Soul that has come to this beautiful city to share his Wisdom on flying free from the mundane to the lofty heights of our True Majesty.

Four Old Men on The Jetty

The day is Silent
It is early morning and the lights of the day begin to glow against the remnants of the night sky
It has rained through the night—the Rain, the Rain, the Glorious Rain—after a long dry summer
The quaint beachside square—generally bustling with life is empty now—save a few of us that join in with the beauty and the Silence—of this special place—at this special time
I watch a man cross-legged on the wet grass—deep in meditation
The runner flies past and we nod in greeting
Beauty and Serenity pervade the Moment
I walk on the jetty
And stand at the point where the Ocean greets the land
What a Special junction this is—where two great forces meet
The Power surges through my body renewing every cell
I look along the beach and watch the waves crashing on the shore—a shore that seems to go forever in the distance
I walk further on the jetty—and watch the four fishermen as they stand in vigil
Ever so patient
Sometimes in Silence
Sometimes exchanging fishing stories about the one they caught and the one that got away
I look at them in their quiet serenity
Perhaps they have a deeper understanding of Life
These four old men fishing
As they stand on the jetty—just Being

Being One with the glorious expanse in front of their eyes
Being One with the jetty
Being One with the fishing rod they so expertly attend to
Being One with each other
The rain drops gently fall and it's Ok for them
It is all part of the experience
They stand on the jetty and nothing else exists for them
For they are in the Moment and all that embraces
—One with their surroundings
—One with the Ocean
—One with the fish
—One with themselves
Four old men on the jetty
And in the Simplicity of their Presence they show us the way
How to Be One with Life
What a Glorious Gift on this silent earth morning on the jetty in front of the quaint beachside square
I thank them for their gift and smile as I leave the jetty and get on with my day.

How Special it is to Be Alive

I sit in a little hamlet high above the plains of the city
A little hamlet tucked away amongst the trees and the wet earth and the beauty of autumn
I sit outdoors—al fresco!—under a large elm tree in a busy little café—eating some delicious wholesome food and sipping on a caffè latte
The spectacular green of the scene is intoxicating
I listen to the baubles of the people around me as they too enjoy the feast in front of their eyes
I watch a baby on the shoulder of a mother
I delight in our Connection as we both beam a smile as he catches my eye
I listen to the birds—so diverse from those at my Beloved Seaside
The air is still and cool
Despite all the activity around me—a Silence pervades the Moment
It slowly moves to the forefront and the scene moves into the distance—taking on a surreal quality
The two worlds coexist
How Delicious this Moment is
I look up and watch a couple sharing a kiss
I smile
They define the Power of this Moment as Life around me baubles along
How Special it is to Be Alive.

I Like Your Trees

It is a perfect morning on a perfect day
The air is crisp and still
The birds quietly bauble their songs
I sit under the magnificent trees in the front yard of my beautiful
home enjoying a delicious breakfast and a wonderful espresso
My home is not far from a kindergarten
And mothers park their cars along the street in front of my home
to take their Precious Little Ones there
It was only a matter of weeks ago that the year started anew
And young ones went on what was for them—a grand new
adventure
Some so excited at the new possibilities in front of them
And some screaming at the top of their young voices

"Mummy/Daddy I want to go Home!!"

Pleading not to be abandoned by their parent
And afraid of the big world outside their familiar surroundings
My Heart felt the pang of fear in their young pleas
And yet who of us would deny them this grand new experience
in their tender young lives
And sometimes—as with these Precious Young Ones—have we
not had Moments in our lives when we scream to the heavens
in fear?
And we are encouraged
Or we are pulled
Or we are pushed—to move
For in the paralysis of not moving forward—we entrench the fear

And do not realize in that Moment
That moving to the next step or the next adventure
Will set us free
As the mother eagle high above the plains pushes its baby out of the nest
For she knows that it has wings and can fly
And that one day it will soar in the heavens
I sip on my espresso under the magnificent trees
And watch a mother help her little one out of the car for her day ahead
As her mother turns her attention to helping her baby brother
—the young child and I share Precious Moments as we smile and we wave to each other
She then whispers something to her mother, who encourages her to share it with me

She turns to me and says *"I like your trees!"*

I wish her well in her day at kindergarten
And I bow and smile in honour to this Precious Young One
In recognition of the depth of her Awareness and Wisdom
My Heart sings and I finish my espresso

"All is Well with the world—All is Well."

It is New Year's Eve and There is Joy in the Air

It is New Year's Eve and there is Joy in the air
I sit on the promenade overlooking the beach
It is dusk and as night settles in, the lights all around me become ever-brighter
—the lights of the city as they curve around the bay
—the beautiful glow from the moon
—the coloured lights of the many families dotted on the beach
The children play with their glow sticks and their glow rings
Their giggles and squeals of laughter are a delight
The myriad of colours and patterns of the fireworks in the suburbs along the shoreline light up the night sky
There is a gentle sea breeze blowing on this most Divine of evenings deep into summer
The night is filled with the sounds of the Moment
—the crashing waves of my Beloved Ocean
—the laughter and squeals of the children as they play
—the muffled sounds of conversations of people as they stroll behind me on the promenade
A couple stop and share greetings and comment that I have the best seat in the house as I sit comfortably in my deckchair and share this Precious Moment with the expanse of the Beauty around me
It is indeed a Precious Moment on a Special day on a Special world
How Blessed We Are
There is excitement in the air as people celebrate as they herald in the new
—New beginnings with new hopes
—New aspirations and
—New journeys to travel

I contemplate the year that has been and the gamut
of emotions I experienced
—As I moved between moments of pure Connection and
moments of disconnection and suffering
—Surfing the waves of this Extraordinary Life we are privileged
to live
I experienced moments of heaven and moments of hell on
this most Precious World
And moments that transcended both
—As I Connected to a Greater Reality
—And Connected to Pure Awareness of my Truth and my
Connection to Life, the Universe, All There Is and beyond
I sang high notes and I sang low notes in this most Divine
Symphony that is our lives
I look to the heavens and it takes my breath away
The clouds high in the night sky streak across the heavens
Are they the wings of Angels who have come to join us on
this most Special of nights?
The stars sheepishly peak through
And the iridescent halo of the Light of our Sun around the
moon adds to the significance of this Magical night
Fireworks set alight from the beach near me light up the sky
I laugh—it feels like my own private show!!
The children on the beach squeal with Delight as the
kaleidoscope of colours burst in front of their eyes on this
Special night in their tender young lives

More fireworks are lit in the distance
What is it about fireworks that delights us—the colours,
the movements, the sparkles, the sounds
They are universally loved by man
Could it be that they stir beautiful and treasured memories
beyond the limitations of our immediate reality?
We have much to be Grateful for on this Divine of nights
On this most Divine of worlds
And we have much to look to forward to
I wonder what adventures the New Year will bring?

Life Caressing Life

I sit here quietly and alone in a restaurant in a large metropolis—sipping on a latte
I am early for a meeting that is to be held here—a meeting deep in the heart of manifested reality
Although it is around sunset time—I do not see the fiery colours of our Beloved Sun as it sinks to the horizon and opens a portal to another world
—I do not feel the wind on my face or feel it tease my skirt as I sit on my Beloved Rocks high above my Beloved Ocean
—I do not watch people as they walk on the sand and watch their dogs play at the shore
I sit in a sad restaurant with artificial lights on a vinyl chair on an artificial carpet
I see the deep, deep chasm between what is enjoyment in the world of Man and what is the Joy of Freedom to Dance with Creation
How many yet sleep and do not recognize the Gap between the two worlds
As I sit in this sad restaurant in a large metropolis somewhere—the Gap appears so large
And yet I know that at the same time it is so small
For True Reality is close—so close—a mere heartbeat away—a mere blink away
I look out the window passing time and a frond on a small palm tree catches my eye as it slowly sways
How curious—it is the only frond moving!

It sways and sways and then I understand and smile as I greet it back
I feel the Life of the palm leaf and for a Moment we Dance as it sways and I sway with it
The Connection Complete
The Moment Full—the Moment Fulfilled
Life Caressing Life
I finish my latte and prepare to go to my meeting in the world of Man and discuss the Oh so important matters of Man!
And as I leave I Smile and Bow to the palm leaf
In acknowledgment and Gratitude.

Life Flowing from Night to Day—
Back to Night—Back to Day

My beautiful uncle has died
On this glorious earth day
As the morning colours slowly awaken
As the birds begin their song
As the fresh morning air refreshes our body, our mind
and our Soul
I take a deep breath and breathe in Life and marvel
at the wonder of it all
One life dies and others awaken
Perhaps the difference is not so great
Perhaps there is no death—there is only Life
Life flowing from night to day—back to night—
back to day
In the endless cycle of this Glorious thing we call Life
Ever changing—ever flowing—ever transmuting
What is the purpose of it all?
What if—it as Simple and as Glorious as the
opportunity to experience Life
Life experiencing Life—how Beautiful—how Special
Rest in Peace dear Uncle—Enjoy your next adventure.

My Heart Sings and My Soul Soars

I sit in a small town high above the plains of the city
I sit on a bench in front of the lovingly manicured gardens
of a quaint small church
The air is clearer here high above the plains
The day is alive and the colours fluoresce in the sunlight
—the spectacular blues of the glorious sky and the vivid
and rich greens of the lush grass
My Spirit lifts and my Soul sings
I have just met with a wonderful Soul helping people in
remarkable ways
What an Extraordinary Journey we travel on this most
Precious of Worlds and meet the most Extraordinary People
I look to the sky and smile as I see what appear to be the
grand wings of Angels and Archangels flying through the
heavens and playing hide and seek with the clouds
A Dear One who has gone through much tribulation has
just shared a snippet of good news—I share in his triumph
And my Heart Sings and my Soul Soars as I give Gratitude
and Celebrate these Precious Moments on this Magnificent Day
in this little patch of Heaven tucked away in the manicured
garden high above the plains.

The Masters Have Arrived

I sit under the magnificent trees in the front yard of my home, having breakfast
It is the time of day when parents escort their Precious Little Ones to the kindergarten nearby
Many of the parents walk by oblivious of my presence
—not having the habit of greeting people as they meet them
How sad—locked in the world of their unconscious minds
And then there are those magical Moments of Connection that take my breath away and my Heart Soars
—and it often comes from the young ones
This morning a father flies by on a bike with a child in the back seat—the child could not be more than three years old
As he flies past the child waves and screams out to me—
"Hiiiiiiiiiii"
I laugh in acknowledgement and return his greeting
The father turns around to see who the child is talking to
and then greets me as he disappears into the distance
Yes!!—the Masters have arrived
All is Well with the World, all is Well
I finish my espresso and skip into my day!!

The Priorities of This Short and Extraordinary Life

I awake to a spectacular morning at that Divine time of the dawn of the day
The clouds begin to glow
The hills in the distance take on a surreal quality as their silhouettes are still shrouded in mist
The air is cold and delicious after days of light rain
The bird sounds are lively this morning—there is an extra joy in their greeting after the rain as they proclaim that All is Well with the World
How Divine their Songs are
I sit on the top balcony watching the ever-brightening glow of the colours of the sky as they herald the sunrise
It is at that special juncture when the Moment is full of potential and excitement of a new day that is rising and yet has not arrived
Today will bring its own special Moments
Celebration Connection and Laughter with family and friends
An interlude from the busy-ness of our lives
And it is in these interludes—when we stop and Connect—that we renew and reset our course back on track to the priorities of this short and extraordinary life we are privileged to live.
For it is in the Moments of Connection that we find our True Joy and Fulfilment.

Their Selfless Love has built Mountains and Bridges across Time and Space

I sit under the canopy of the two large evergreen oak trees
—the Magnificent Trees at my family home
—as I eat a delicious breakfast and sip on my espresso coffee
I Rejoice as the contentment soaks through my Being
These Glorious Trees shading the front of the Magnificent Home that my parents built Oh! so long ago
—a mere seven years after coming to this beautiful land
Poor peasants from a village in Italy
These trees that my father so Lovingly planted and Nurtured throughout his life
His Vision has Endured
And as I sit under the Magnificent Trees shading the Magnificent Home
—I think of my parents and smile with Gratitude for all they were and all I have gained from them
For their Selfless Love has built mountains and bridges across time and space
Mountains and bridges that cannot be eroded for they are built from Pure Love—the Fabric of Creation—Selfless, Unconditional and Timeless
What a Beautiful Legacy they have left me—pointing the road Home
I smile and bow in Gratitude for the gifts they gave me and this beautiful world as I finish my espresso and prepare to join the Day.

We Are All Children of this Magnificent World

It is a warm balmy night on the other side of the world
I sit with the breeze caressing my face
I am at the outdoor pool of the hotel
It is twilight and the colours of night are settling in
I watch a young child in the pool with his father
The sight of their playing and teasing and the sounds of their giggling and laughter are delightful and uplifting
The child's mother watches on
I hear the noise of the traffic on the busy freeway nearby
It is Saturday night and the city is bustling with people on their way to somewhere
How curious—as I flew into this city it reminded me of my own Beloved country and the cities of my country
So much is similar
And yet there are differences—for here there is a melting pot of races different to those in my country
And although I see the differences—as I hear the laughter and the excitement in the voices of the people and watch them interact with each other—I realize that the similarity of people overrides the differences
For we are all Children of this Magnificent World
And we all sing a song and have longings in our Heart
And we all have those who Love us and those who care and those we Love and those we care for
So this city on the other side of the globe to my Beloved country reveals a Truth—that our differences are small—and it is the gap of understanding that is large—the understanding of the Truth of our similarity

This not about 'sameness' for we are all Unique Extraordinary Beings
This is about the similarity in our Collective Humanity at its highest levels of ideals and potential
We all have visions and dreams and desires and longings and the drive to forge forward and bring these into Reality for ourselves and those we Love
And as our Wisdom grows—it is these things that we understand and appreciate with greater clarity
—and that Humanity beats with One Heartbeat
And as we continue to grow in Wisdom— we understand and appreciate with Greater Clarity
—that Humanity and the all the animals of Earth beat with One Heartbeat
And as we continue to grow in Wisdom—we understand and appreciate with Greater Clarity
—that All on this extraordinary world hurtling through space, Humanity and all the animals and the plants and All Living things beat with One Heartbeat
And as we continue to grow in Wisdom—we understand and appreciate with Greater Clarity
—that All on this extraordinary Jewel of a World and All in this extraordinary Universe that is our home beats with One Heartbeat
What an Extraordinary Life we Live.

We Have Much to Celebrate and Much to Look Forward To

I sit in a busy square in a busy metropolis
It is that wonderful hour on a Friday night when work is out and the mood is high and people walk with a spring in their step and a spring in their voice as if to say
"Yes!! Free for the weekend"
The temperature is perfect on a Divine balmy night
The square is spacious and modern
Created by the genius of man
With modern pavements, steps, seats, sculptures and statues
The bronze lions, a symbol of power, take centre stage in front of the city hall which stands tall and proud
Other bronze statues that adorn the square celebrate the wonderful pioneering spirit and pioneering history of the area
A large screen in a corner of the square beams out the latest cricket match—India vs Australia—*"Hey, Australia just scored another run!"*
During an interval of the match, the symphony orchestra and the ballet company of the city proudly showcase their culture
There is so much loving attention in the creation of this beautiful modern hamlet in the city
The square bustles with activity at this wonderful hour of the day
—as commuters beeline their way home after a day cloistered in one of the buildings
—or hover and chit-chat the important talk of the moment
The tourists sit and enjoy and take photos with the statues—
lest they forget this Precious Moment in time
A father and young daughter play chasey around the square and the child squeals with delight as she outmanoeuvres him

A corner of the square captivates my attention
—with the familiar sounds of Friday night Happy Hour—indeed
—as people stand or sit and chat and laugh and delight in this
Precious time out
Freedom!!—maybe only from the tedium of the week and only for a
weekend however in this moment—it is Freedom
A small step it may be—nevertheless a step it is—The Soul Celebrates
I meander over and join them—in the modern alfresco restaurant—
The Groovy Train—Hah, hah!!—but of course!!
The sounds of Life bubble all around me as people drink, eat and
share their stories and their lives in this interlude on this glorious
evening
The singer-guitarist adds his soulful harmonies
A Divine Moment in a Divine City on a Divine Day
A Moment treasured forever in my memories of this beautiful place
on this most Beautiful of Worlds
The colours of the day slowly fade and the colours of the city begin
to light up and merge with the colours of the sky as night settles in
The City Hall is lit up and showcases the ideals of the city and the
struggles that made the city great
It stands magnificent and proud with its sentinel of lions and against
the backdrop of the modern tall skyscrapers

"I will survive, I will survive" sings the singer—indeed!!

As a people, we have roads yet to travel and understandings yet
to gain

Cont ...

And yet—like this Friday night—we can Pause for a Moment and Enjoy
For we have Much to be Proud of
And Much to be Grateful for
And Much to Celebrate on the roads we have travelled
And Much to Look Forward to on the roads yet to be explored
As I sit and enjoy the baubles of Life around me in this beautiful city—I ponder in this moment the Connection between all peoples
For this could be any city on this Beautiful World
As people come together and Share Precious Moments in the interludes of their lives

And the singer sings
"I just want you to know who I am"
and *"Alleluia-Alleluia"*

Hah hah!! He knows!!
We have much to Celebrate
And the Angels Join In.

Who and What Will You Be in This Game of Life?

The days go by—One Moment at a time
The seconds incessantly tick by—forever marching to the future—
but never reaching it
Our brain in a whirlwind of activity—trying to make sense of it all
Forever in motion—linking the past, the present and the future
Or so it believes
Trying to make Sense of it all
As the moments of our lives tick, tick, tick, tick incessantly by
We were born in this reality—the choice not ours—or so it seems!!
And feel the incessant urge to make sense of it all
Thinking that if we somehow make sense of it all—it will change?
Or we will control it—and then change it?
Or we can just relax and accept it
That these are the parameters of this reality
—like the parameters of a video game
These are the rules—so what?
What can we achieve within these parameters?
Pretty cool really—an adventure in this particular sim reality
So—Who and What will You Be in this Game of Life?

PART FOUR
....

The Journey of the Soul

A New Phase Begins

It is sunset and I sit in the front yard of my beautiful home
It is the end of a most challenging time
I now sit and breathe the glorious air of a New Moment and a New Phase
I hear the birds sing their sweet songs again
And see the brilliant majesty of our most Divine Sun
Its Light streams on my face and a Peace flows over me
A New Phase begins
It felt like the challenges of the phase just ended were
old ways fighting for survival
And attempting to frustrate my jump into the new
They arose one after the other—seemingly in a never-ending stream
At times I triumphed
And at times I sank beneath the waves of anxiety and despair
For I thought that phase had ended—and it had not
I was being challenged again with old and obsolete ways
And yet, I now sit with the Sun streaming on my face
And I Know—that phase has indeed ended
And I have Triumphed
For now, I rest and give Thanks for all that have helped me through the trials
I breathe the fresh air of the New
I know other challenges will arise

And so it is on this Grand Journey—spiralling ever
Onwards and Upwards
Right now, I relish in this Glorious Moment
As I swim in the Divine sunset and as our most Precious
Sun streams on my face
I Smile
And I give Thanks for this Extraordinary Journey of Life
on this Beautiful World that is Our Home.

A Point of Connection Between God and Man

It is early morning and a cool breeze blows along the shore
I walk between the Ocean and the sand dunes
The beach is mine—only I am walking this secluded stretch of beach
The Moment—Divine and Intimate
Time ceases
The Ocean, the Divine Ocean is Home for me
I adore it beyond adoration and Love it completely
I walk along the shore and watch each wave with its white caps as it greets the land
I Am Home as I Merge with the Ocean
I watch a wave as it rolls in and feel the wave and feel each wave and feel the Ocean beneath the waves
I become each wave and all the waves and the Ocean all at the same time
How curious, I think back to a time I was asked what is my passion and struggled to answer
—Until I realized that my Connection with the Ocean is beyond passion
—That it is such a part of My Being that I never recognized it outside of myself
The Ocean courses through my veins—it is part of My Soul
I walk along the edge of the shore and play a game with the Ocean that
I have played as long as I remember
As a wave rolls to the shore, I walk at the edge I believe the wave will end
Sometimes I win and sometimes the Ocean wins
I Laugh with Delight
Many a times I have gone home with wet shoes!!
I Treasure a memory of a time when I walked on the beach
with a Kindred Soul and to my absolute Delight he also played
the game—only he was masterful at it!!

I wonder if there is something more profound in this gesture beyond a silly little pastime
Perhaps like Michelangelo's fresco of The Creation
—It is a Point of Connection between God and Man
There is a Profound Intimacy at the point when I touch the tip of the wave, the tip of the Ocean
—A Moment of Divine Connection
And So I walk the beach and I look up at the clouds
The glorious clouds so white against the azure blue of the spectacular sky
A pelican effortlessly glides by
And the seagulls fly past, back from their sleeping nests
Every evening at sunset they fly north and every morning they fly back
So easy—no thought—no agonizing over what to do
They just do what they do
Perhaps there is gift in this for us
And So I walk between the Ocean and the sand dunes
Time has stood still and this Moment is Eternal
I Am Home.

An Infinitesimal Probability—And Yet, We Are Here!!

The night Divine
The moon shines brightly in the night sky—the stars dim in the background
I sit on the patio of my second-story balcony and relish in the beauty in front of my eyes
The misty spray of water from the giant sprinklers on the oval is cool and delicious
A vapour trail from a jet high in the night sky luminesces in the light of the night and appears to define the curvature of the earth—high above and low to the horizon on either side
It is but an illusion of what it appears to represent
—however it still tantalizes the mind
A reminder that we are on this beautiful ball of rock hurtling through space
What an Extraordinary Life we live
The cars on the road in the distance are mesmerizing
—Life in Motion
A distant plane comes in over the hills to land at the nearby airport of our most beautiful city
I marvel at the Wonder of it all
To be witnessing myself observing Life around me
And to be part of the Life observing Life—observing Itself
Wow!! What are the chances to have reached this possibility?
An infinitesimal probability—and yet we are here!!
We have much to Celebrate.

And So It Flows—In Infinity, From Infinity

A spectacular night
The Silence goes forever
We are deep into the night
The Moment Divine
The ground wet from drizzle not long ago
The night crisp and cool
The air is still
Nothing stirs—the lack of noise deafening
The full moon shines in the heavens reflecting the Light of the
Sun deep into the night and lighting up the world
The few clouds hang in the sky and touch the ground with their
reflection on the river—still as a mirror
A distant sound of crickets
The street lights in the distance pierce the night
The orange lights of a freeway define the hills as it curves
its way up
The Glow of the light at this Divine hour casts the shadows of
the trees on the mirrored river—a perfect reflection
Man sleeps
There is not a sound from his world but for the distant drone
of a car engine on a faraway road
The bridge now glows red
The Stars—pinpoints of Light—scatter across the night sky
How do I describe this Sacred Moment?
It defies containment and defies description and defies analysis—
for these are the limited constructs of the human
mind
And this Moment is beyond the capacity of the human mind
An answer comes

"Come My Beautiful One Come
Open your heart and open your mind and release your will
Let go of what you think I Am
Let go of your description of me for that is but the appearance
Surrender to my Truth and you will experience me as I will experience you—making Love at its most profound"

And so I release the beauty of the night and open My Heart and open My Mind and open My Soul to the Truth beyond the beauty
And I feel the Pulse of Life beating beneath it
And then I go beyond the beat of the Pulse
And as I dive into the Silence I expect to rest in Stillness—in pure Intelligence—in pure Awareness
But I go beyond it
I go to where the Silence is dynamic and it oscillates between stillness and creation and I oscillate with it
And Life Force is created by the oscillation—Life Force that sustains the world that we know
And so behind the Silence there is dynamic Flow and behind the dynamic Flow there is Silence
And so it flows
—In Infinity, from Infinity
—In Eternity, from Eternity
In Deep Gratitude I sit—in Silence
And the full moon shines overhead—and the liquid darkness of the night is pierced by the Stars and the lights of man
And the crisp, cool early morning air
And the river mirrors the world above
How Divine
Life in Silence—Life in Motion.

And So the Ripples Expand Across Creation

The day flows from idea to Divinity
From beauty to what next
The day flows with me or without me
What would my day be if it flowed from the power of my
Attention and the power of my Desires?
What beautiful world would manifest before my eyes if I
Consciously Choose my desires and Will them into the world
as the Creator Willed us into Being?
What world would I Create?
Would it be as Beautiful as the Jewel of our beautiful blue-green home?
Would it be as Beautiful as our co-travellers, the animals and plants and all living things that inhabit it?
Would it be as Beautiful as the Magnificent Bodies that we inhabit on this Magnificent World?
And the answer comes

"How could it be otherwise my Beautiful Ones
For you a Creation born of Pure Love
And if you will your Creation from the Love and Joy that You Are
Your Creation will carry the seeds of the Divine
And your Creation will be as Beautiful as You Are"

And so the Ripples Expand Across Creation
"Welcome Home my Beautiful Ones, Welcome Home."

And There Will Be Much Celebration in the Heavens and on Earth

The Divine morning Sun bursts over the horizon
Its splendour bursts into the day and lifts the darkness from the night and the heaviness from my Heart
Sadness at the heavy pain of Dear Ones as their journeys take separate roads
All is the hands of the Divine and at this time they cannot see the Joy that awaits them in the new
They are at the Moment of the night just before the breaking dawn not realizing what is to come
That Moment that is full of anticipation of what is about to unfold
That Moment as the night begins to fade and you wait in Stillness—for the Sun will soon burst over the horizon and the nightmares of the night will be dissolved in the power of its Light
I will offer them support on their journey in this time of challenge as they walk their roads to their dawn
I was blessed with support of Loved Ones in dark days on my journey
In the darkness, a position of loss is traumatizing as we cling in fear and insecurity to familiar relationships or familiar situations or familiar possessions in a desperate attempt to buffer ourselves from the pain
And now as I watch the rising Sun burst forth and Bless this world with Life, I know I Am wealthy beyond measure
For all the gold on this planet is but a drop in the Ocean of my True Wealth

For I sit at the table of the Divine
And I share in the True Riches of this Beautiful World
—Stunning beyond measure
—As I Dance with Life around me—our Glorious Sun, the wind, the blue of the sky, my Beloved Ocean, the glorious colours and sounds and the feel of Life as it pulses around me and through me
—And as I experience the Infinite well of my Truth—the Truth of Light and Beauty and Joy and Love and the pulse and wonder of Life and Creation
I will gently remind them of their Truth as I was gently reminded of mine on this Glorious Journey
And I await that Moment when they too will stand in the fading darkness of the night and watch their Sun burst over the horizon and bathe their world in the splendour of their Light
And there will be much Celebration in the Heavens and on Earth.

Are You Enjoying Our Dance?

The new has commenced
Not with a whisper, but with a sounding of trumpets and the singing of Angels as the Heavens herald another of its own Home
The prodigal children returning to the place of their birth from adventures through time
They have walked the fires of hell and swam the swamps and cried through the night in agony and despair as a Soul is lost in the fabric of Time and Space
They have experienced pain and misery and despair beyond endurance on their journey through the darkness
And their screams were heard throughout the Heavens
—and both Heaven and Earth wept
But even in the darkest of Moments whether they saw it or not, felt it or not, knew it or not—a Light always shone—the Light of their Truth, ever pointing the road Home
And so the children slowly claw their way out of the darkness—showing flashes of Brilliance along the way—acts of Courage, Moments of Insight, Love amongst the ashes, Beauty in the midst of the agonising pain
And in these Moments they shine the Light in a dark world
If only they knew the power of these achievements—they change reality forever
And so Man walks the road towards his Truth
A long, difficult, tedious road—not knowing the next steps, not knowing what is over the hill or around the corner
But slowly, each step is crawled and each step brings the Soul closer, ever closer to Home

And with each step, the journey becomes Lighter, ever so faintly
As Wisdom and Knowing grows in the Heart of Man
And Compassion and Understanding and Laughter and Joy
The Journey Lightens ever so slightly
And the Soul awakens, ever so gently, ever so lovingly amidst the carnage of the past
And slowly and gently the Light brightens and their eyes lift to the Truth of their Being and the Truth of the magnificent world around them
And in that awakening recognition, both God and Life are Glorified
And the Love they begin to know they are, they begin to recognize in all Life around them
And they start to Dance
Joyously, passionately, completely, totally they Dance
They Dance across Time and Space
They Dance with Life
They Dance the Dance of Life
And their eyes turn to Heaven and they smile for they Know
Man and the Divine dancing the Sacred Dance of Life together
Pirouetting across Time and Space
Pirouetting across Time and Eternity

"Hello my Beautiful Ones—Welcome Home
 What a Joy You Are
 Have You enjoyed your grand adventure?
 Are You Enjoying Our Dance?"

As the Soul Walks from its Night to the Dawn

Sadness fills my Heart
To feel the suffering of those around me
Would I ease their pain—would I ease their burden
And yet I too walked the road they now walk
The pain of the Heart and the pain of the Soul—lost in the world of Man
Aching for its Truth
Aching to feel its own Love
Aching to feel its own Gentleness
Aching to feel its own Purpose
Aching to feel its own Joy
Aching to feel its own Life
Aching to feel its own Divinity
And yet—there is Celebration
For in feeling the pain they are on their road Home
Till this point they were asleep—oblivious to the effect of their actions
The pain is experienced as they awaken
As they experience the realization of their Life till then
Their misguided perceptions and actions and the understanding of the suffering resulting from them
Although the pain is great there is Celebration in the Heavens
As the Soul walks from its night to the dawn
And in this painful time we offer our Encouragement and Love
For soon they will walk into the Brilliance of their own day
Into the Brilliance of their own Light

And they will give thanks for the journey they had travelled
And the pain and the sorrow and the suffering will fade as a distant nightmare
As it is replaced with the Joy and the beauty of Life and the sweetness of their own Being
As they Live in the Truth of their own Light and their own Brilliance.

Bring Your Truth to this Beautiful Realm and Watch Miracles Happen

What does it all mean—these senseless games that humans play?
Filling the Precious Moment with self-importance
Seemingly so critical to one's self-image
Seemingly so vital to one's defense of the construct of the mind
The false reality defended to the end
The illusion defended with all one's breath
What senseless pastimes
Would you defend a shadow on the wall?
Such defenses are meaningless to the Truth—instead creating pain and havoc and sorrow
They can achieve nothing real—for they are not True Reality
All outside of Self are mere shadows on the wall
And yet you defend them to the end—attempting to impose a meaning beyond its Truth

"Do you not see Dear Ones that your short life will end soon enough?
And then where are all your points of view you defended so strongly?
They have evaporated for they were never real
Place your attention Dearest Ones on Your Truth
Concern yourselves not with attack or defense of your perception of the Truth or illusion of others for this is not your concern
Bring Your Truth to this beautiful realm—and watch Miracles happen
For in that Moment you will recognize the Truth of all Creation
And you will Dance the Dance of Life—and Creation will Dance the Dance of your Truth
The rest is trivial until such time—taking up your Precious Attention and your Sacred Journey

*The only way you can realize your dreams and your desires—
for yourself and your Loved Ones and your Beautiful home
you call Earth—is to Live your Truth
And for all else give Unconditional Love and Unconditional
Non-judgement—for this will set both you and they free
This my Dearest Ones is the road Home
And the Greatest Gift you can offer your fellow man and
all Life that co-exists with you on your beautiful world
and beyond."*

Connection to the Grand Universe Beyond

The depth of the night entrancing
The sounds of man barely a distant drone—like ripples
on a still pond
The cool air barely a waft of a breeze
The moon barely a yellow sliver as it hangs in the night sky
All is still
The Silence goes Forever
The night belongs to the Stars
Portals of Light in the depths of dark space
Their Presence lift our eyes to the Heavens
Away from our ordinary little lives
To the Truth of our real Home amongst the Stars
I look at each Star and wonder about its Life
I feel their Connection across time and space
A Connection to the Grand Universe beyond
Their Truth is larger than the capacity of our brain to
hold it
And yet at some level I do hold it
At some level I do comprehend the Truth of the Stars
At some level I know their Life
And I know their Story
And I know their Beauty
And I know their Power
And I know their Wonder
For every atom in my Being was forged in the Stars
Through the endless cycle of Life and Death that they too
are a part of

And every atom of my Being carries the Memory of its Journey
And as I look up to the Stars a Memory stirs
For without them I would not exist
And my story is not complete without their story
And as I look at the Stars—I smile
For I remember Who I Am
And the wondrous Journey I have travelled in this Beautiful Universe that is our Home

*"And if the mundane pressures of everyday Life weigh you down
Look up to the Stars in the Heavens and remember your Glorious Journey
And that this Life you are now living, on this beautiful planet we call Earth
Is but a small snippet of a far Grander Adventure."*

Hundredfold to the Power of Infinity

The days are long—the stress traumatizing in the density of ignorance in our reality
I can see and yet I am blind
I can touch and yet I do not feel
I can hear and yet I do not comprehend
The chaos and confusion of straddling two worlds
I see the beauty and underneath the ugliness of our behaviour to Life on this most special of worlds
I hear the chirp of the birds and underneath hear the agonizing screams of the animals we kill so brutally in their billions each year
I feel the caress of the wind on my face and underneath feel the brutal and destructive exploitation of man to all on this
Jewel of a World
I close my eyes and feel the Peace of the Moment and feel the tears of Mother Earth as we tear her apart and all living things that inhabit her
My tears fall silently in the Moment

"Do you not see Dearest Ones?
The destruction you wreak upon others you feel as well
The pain you cause others you feel as well
The senseless exploitation you cause in the name of power you feel as well
How else, My Dearest Ones, when you do not truly feel and do not know will you realize that All is One?

That the Heart that beats in your Brother and the Heart that beats in the Animals and the Heart that beats in the Trees and the Heart that beats in the Ocean—Is Your Heart
Would you knowingly rip out Your Heart to find that which you seek?
And what do you seek My Loved Ones—is it not Love and Peace and Joy and Freedom?
Respect this in the world around you and you will receive it Hundredfold to the Power of Infinity
It is Your actions that determine Your Reality—not what you believe is going on around you
For in Truth there is Only One
In Truth there is only You."

Is The Breeze Touching Me or Am I Touching the Breeze?

The night is dark
The sounds muffled in the distance
The night still warm from a hot day
There is something about an evening after a long hot day
—a languishing after the stifling heat
I sit on the top balcony relishing in the freedom of outdoors—after a day of being cloistered in four walls
The tightness in my body begins to melt as I sit in the Expanse of the night
The boundaries so familiar in the light of day disappear into the night
What a Glorious time this is—when the constant bombardment of the input to the senses during the day dissolves into the night
And is replaced with a heightened Awareness of the Reality around me
How curious as my mind quietens—I experience more, not less—
I feel more, not less—and my awareness grows, not diminishes
My Delight in this Moment grows as I tune in to the Life pulsing around me—as the clutter and chaos of the overload of the day fades
An eddy of a breeze wafts by—how delicious it is as it tantalizes my skin
Is the breeze touching me or am I touching the breeze?
Or is it a Dance between both?
The sounds of the night come to the forefront—the crickets—the sound of water from the large sprinklers on the lawn of the oval—
the occasional car on the road in the distance
I look up at the sky and my Heart melts—it has been too long
—caught in the frenetic pace of modern urban existence—since I looked to the Stars

I breathe deep and sink back into my chair—as I realign to the
Truth of the stunning Reality around me
As I Connect to the Reality around me—it Connects to me
And the Connection becomes seamless—as our Truths merge into
One Truth
The Truth of the expression of Life
The Truth of the expression of Reality
The Truth of the expression of the Divine as it plays in this
Glorious Wonderland of Creation
What a Privilege Life Is.

It Sings, We Sing—We Sing, It Sings

The morning colours slowly rise in the peace of the morning
Slowly they rise
As the world slowly rises from its slumber
As the birds begin their song
As man slowly awakens from his dreams
Slowly and silently the day moves forward
Life in motion
We live our lives—the birds live their lives—the Earth lives its life—the Sun lives its life—and so on it goes
And together we interact and share and communicate across the divides
We may not even know we are doing it
Or know that our well-being is intricately woven with Life we share on this extraordinary world that we are a part of
And that we gain nourishment, sustenance, Life Force and Joy from
What would our lives be without the rising colours of the dawn?
What would our lives be without the silhouettes of the majestic trees?
What would our lives be without the sound and glorious sight of birds in flight?
Our well-being is finely tuned to the world around us
It Thrives, we Thrive—we Thrive, it Thrives
It Sings, we Sing—we Sing, it Sings
Feel the Life Force course through your Being in the Presence of a rising dawn
Feel the Wonder in your eyes as you watch the flight of an albatross
Feel the Delight as you splash in the waves of the Ocean
Feel the Majesty of Life as you look at the Stars in the night sky

The wellness of our Life on all levels is intricately woven in the fabric of the Creation we are a part of
And with the wellness of all the Life we travel with on this wondrous journey through Creation
What an extraordinary Dance across time and space
And what an extraordinary opportunity as humans to Consciously share our Life Force in Gratitude for the Life Force of All around us
Life Force that nourishes us
And we have the awareness to Consciously Choose to nourish Life in return
And All that embraces and All that means
And so we pirouette Onwards and Upwards in this extraordinary Dance of Life that we are privileged to share.

Keep Your Desires Alive

The full moon shines brightly—lighting up the Heavens and
the Earth with the intoxicating Light of our Divine Sun
The cool breeze Delicious on the body
The Ripples on the river shine in the Light
Life in Motion—the Ripples of Creation
It is late and the traffic has eased and then almost
miraculously it stops
What a Gift from Heaven
I smile and skip down the centre of the road again for what
seems an Eternity and not one vehicle passes to disturb the
Silence
My Delight is palpable and my Joy delightful as we share this
Gift again
How curious, I remember the sadness I experienced at what
I thought would be the loss of the Silence once the bridge
was reopened
And yet—here it is again
A Gap in the chaos of traffic
A Gap in the Chaos of Time
A Gap—when the spectacular beauty of the full Moon and the
dark velvety night and the intoxicating cool breeze—and the
Silence of the elements—rule the Moment

*"Dearest Ones do you not understand that All is Possible—for the
Creation of Reality occurs beyond the realm of Man not within it
So keep your Desires alive—for you never know when they manifest—
in the blink of an eye all can change*

So what do you Desire my Dearest Ones for Yourself?
And what do you Desire for your Loved Ones?
And what do you Desire for your community?
And what do you Desire for your planet and all your co-travellers
on your beautiful world?
For this Dearest Ones is the first step in Creating the world of
your dreams
And manifestation spontaneously arises and flows from your Creation
So what does it take to Create the world of your Dreams?
It takes the first step—and another first step—and another first step
For you can Create your Desires in every Moment of every day of your
most Precious Existence on your most Precious Home you call Earth."

Know Your Truth

How do I jump this chasm that separates me from my Truth?
A chasm that seems impossible to jump and impossible to cross
Separating me from my world that I see so clearly and that awaits me
The Truth that is who I Am
The World that is my Right
The World that is my Contribution and my Legacy and my Joy and my Fulfilment
The World I have dreamed about in the depth of the nightmares
The World that has kept me moving—moving towards it even when all seems lost
The World that gives me Hope amongst the despair
The World that I know will bring Love and Joy to All on this beautiful world
Now that I am close—so close—I can see it and feel it and taste it—it pervades all my senses
I know it is my Birthright
I know it is my Truth
I know I Am so close
I am at the edge of the chasm that separates me from All that I Am—and All that I have Dreamed about all these aeons—and All that I can Be
So Here I Am—what Now?
The anxiety of its Presence but not its fulfilment fills me with impatience and frustration and a hunger—not of what it is, but that I am not reaching it and all that I know awaits

"So what do I need to do?" I beam across the Heavens

And the answer comes

"Do nothing—for it is not in the Doing
 Be All—for this is the Path to your Truth
 Be that which you see and know to be You at its most Grandest
 Step into your Greatness—and know this is who You Are
 The Key does not rest in the world of Man but in the World of the Divine—your birthright
 Know your Truth
 And the chasm will dissolve before your eyes—for in Truth it does not exist—it is a construct of the world of Man
 Trust your Divinity—and Trust your Truth—and Trust your Greatness
 And the World of Creation will unfold in front of You
 And Your Dreams will Manifest like Child's play
 For the Wonder of All and the Glory of your Beautiful World
 Glory be to You in the Highest and in the World of Man
 Amen."

Let The Dance Begin

The journey begins
It begins now
There is nothing left to do
There is nothing left to complete
All is in readiness
All not done has lost its significance
All yet to do has faded into oblivion
All is ready for the New
The head is turned to Home
A time that we have prepared for ever since coming to this most Precious World
Thanks are given, goodbyes are said—and all is now ready for the New
A Life so Glorious it was not even imagined in the past
These times are much misunderstood in history
Do you leave the body? That is not the question
What you do leave is your old world behind—attachments that you held on for dear life in the past now seem so unimportant
So your world changes
Your priorities change, your vision changes, your breathing changes, your friends change, your every cell changes—and you become unrecognizable to the old
Your head and your Heart are firmly planted in your New Direction

Your Heart flutters with excitement at the Glorious World you are entering and soon your memories of your old world and your old ways will fade into the distance like a bad dream of old
Thank it, Bless it for all it has given you—and now say goodbye
For that world and its ways no longer serve you
There is nothing left in common and the connection disappears
And like a line cast off the shore, the ship slowly sails away to the horizon until that shore is but a memory and even then that fades

"So Welcome—Welcome to your New Life
It is more magical that you could know or could even dream of
Let the Dance Begin."

Life is a Destination

I awake from a troubled sleep and a troubled mind
I go outside to break the heaviness of my nightmares and am greeted with the profound Beauty of the Moment
It takes my breath away—for I had forgotten who I AM and how Beautiful this World is
I breathe deep and step into another world as I reconnect to the Magnificence of my Truth and the Truth around me
The night is still
It is early morning and the Earth sleeps
Not a sound can be heard, but for the distant drone of a lonely car
It had been raining and the night is fresh and alive
I breathe deep and revitalize my mind, as the troubles that weighed so heavily lift and dissolve in the Beauty of the Moment
The clouds luminesce in the early morning sky
The profound Silence is Delicious
How curious—all sleep at this hour of the morning—the humans, the animals, the plants
The world and its inhabitants rest from the frenetic pace and the frenetic race
But a race to where?
For we have already arrived
Life is a Destination
And in our ignorance we treat it as a nuisance on the way to somewhere else
The rain starts to gently fall and each drop proclaims its Presence with its gentle sound as it reaches the ground

I wonder what stories the rain could tell on its journeys around the globe
How profoundly Beautiful is this Moment
Complete unto itself
Complete unto its purpose
Complete
And how privileged am I to be a part of it
A magpie commences its magical song far in the distance
Its musical notes drift in the night
And add to the Symphony of Silence and to the Symphony of Life in this magical Moment on this Most Divine of Worlds.

Life is Life and You are All One

It is late afternoon after the end of a hot day
I am eager for the rain that we were told would come
It has been two weeks since it last rained and the earth and the trees and all living things eagerly await the Life-giving sustenance
Without rain we perish
And then it comes—large drops at first and then the Heavens open and the sweet nectar falls to Earth
We all breathe a sigh of relief
—the Rain, the Rain, the Glorious Rain
And then the lightening splits the sky—its awesome power beyond the small ego of Man

"Where is your perceived power now Dearest Ones?
—It pales into insignificance in the Presence of the lightening"

Then thunder booms overhead as clouds crash into each other

"Where is your ego now Dearest Ones?—the grand power you believe you wield
—It pales into insignificance in the Presence of the thunder
And have you been at the effect of a cyclone?
—Where is your power then Dearest Ones?
And have you been in the Ocean at the effect of waves a thousand feet high?
—Where is your power then Dearest Ones?
Is it not clear to you that the human race was not the maker of this glorious world?
And nor do you have the capacity to do so

So why My Dearest, is it so difficult for you to understand that destructive egocentric power upsets the fine balance of Life on your planet?
And in doing so wreaks havoc on all living things
You do not rule Creation—you are a part of it!
Your profound lack of understanding of how your planet is finely tuned
—Does not give your ignorance permission to believe that you have not profoundly upset the balance on your world
—And that you can excuse your behaviour and believe that the rise in calamities, both natural and otherwise, has nothing to do with you
What ignorance My Dearest Children
Do you not see the Earth is a Gift for you and all who inhabit it?
Treasure the Gift and Respect all Life
For in Truth—the Life that created the lightning bolt and the Life that flows through the animals and the trees and all living things is the same Life that courses through Your Being
As you come of age My Dearest Ones you will understand that as you have the capacity to wreak havoc on your world in your ignorance
—You also have the capacity to create Heaven on Earth in your Truth
When of Choice—you Respect your World instead of pillaging it
When of Choice—you Honour your World instead of vilifying it and the beautiful Life that share it with you
When of Choice— you Love your World and all Life that share it with you
And in that Glorious Moment you will feel the Love that all Life has for you
And in that Glorious Moment you will understand that Life is Life and You Are All One
We await that Glorious Day."

My Words Expand Into the Night and Flow into Infinity

The scene surreal, the night magical
The full moon—a super moon—dominates the cloudless night sky
The stars pale into insignificance
The night is cool and the night is silent
The Ocean is still—not a ripple stirs
I sit on the jetty over the point where the sea and the land meet
And watch the waves gently caress the shore and hear their magical sound as they greet each other
The lights of man sparkle in the distance as they light up the shoreline as it curves around the bay
A small plane flies in over the Ocean—its head turned to home
A spectacular scene
A Magical Moment—when man can Touch Infinity
The Infinite Light of our Sun as it reflects off the full moon and Lights up the darkness of the night
The Infinite panorama of the Ocean as it spreads to the horizon
The Infinite depths of space
The Infinite Light of the Stars
The Silence
I grapple with words to share a Moment and a scene and an experience which is beyond words
A scene so complete it defies description
A scene that wraps me in its Beauty—envelopes me—and includes me in its Truth
And what I do and where I live and the circumstances of my life disappear into irrelevance

I stand here enveloped by the Truth of this Moment
—in my Essence, in my Truth
And both share and witness the fullness of Reality
And in this Moment—I understand the Power and the Privilege
of Being Human as I proclaim

"My God how Beautiful"

And my words expand into the night and Flow into Infinity

"Do you now understand, my beautiful children, why it was created?"

Nothing is Lost

A Glorious day unfolds before my eyes
The rain started early this morning
I give Gratitude for the Divine Nectar from the Heavens—the Nectar of Life on our Beautiful World
So appreciated as the temperature rises as a prelude to a long, hot, dry summer
The rain started lightly and then moved into its stride
How Delicious it feels as it falls on my hair
It is mid-morning and I sit on the top balcony enjoying an espresso and enjoying the spectacular play of the Elements around me
We are in an interlude—a calm
The rain has ceased for the Moment
And the Symphony of bird songs rises all around me
There is a sweetness in their tune as they enjoy the rain and all that it offers
I look to the grey clouds so high in the sky—rising to skirt the hills in the distance—they luminesce in the Light of day as they scurry on their journey
I watch as the rain pours from the Heavens far in the distance—silhouetted against a patch of blue sky
The thunder, ever-present, ominously rumbles around me and the flashes of lightning pierce through the clouds
What a privilege it is to experience the Play and the Song of Nature and the Elements—the thunder, the lightening, the rain
—The Rain, the Rain, the Glorious Rain
What memories do they carry across time and space as they sing their tune across billions of years on this most special of worlds?
What stories of their journeys do they hold?

Water—the Nectar of Life—travelling from the far reaches of space to incubate and grow Life on our most Precious Home
What stories can it tell?
Our bodies are mainly Water—and that Precious Water in me resonates to the Rain and resonates to the Ocean and resonates to the memories that Water carries within its Essence—for Nothing is Lost
So as I contemplate the journeys of Water across billions of years of time and from the dark reaches of space—something in me stirs—and I smile and the Joy rises within as I add it to my memories as a human Life on this most Beautiful of Worlds
And so it is for the Carbon and the Oxygen and all the atoms that make up my Being
What stories do they carry from their beginning in a long-lost star billions of years ago?
And so as I Connect to the Power of the Elements and this amazing world—
I smile as I resonate to the myriad of journeys they have travelled since time immemorial and are ever-present, pulsing all around me and within me in the Glorious Living canvas that is this Moment—revealing their stories—and so adding to my memories and my journeys on this wondrous world and beyond
In this most Glorious expression of Divine Life in manifested Reality
What an extraordinarily Privilege it is to be a part of it
And what an extraordinary Privilege it is to experience it
And what an extraordinary Privilege it is to have the Consciousness to know it!!

Ourselves Calling us Home

On this beautiful earth morning I awake to a misty world
A world that appears surreal from the one I know
I walk on the beach next to my Beloved Ocean
The feeling is eerie and yet comforting and familiar as I see only the immediate surroundings and the rest of the world disappears into the mist
If I did not know this place I would have no idea what is beyond the mist
I was at the top of Schilthorn one time—at the top of the world in Switzerland—amongst the mist
In a revolving restaurant seating four hundred, there were only six of us from the corners of the globe—we threw snowballs on the helipad
The mist was thick and we could not see beyond our immediate surroundings
Having never been there I had no idea what lay beyond
That was our world—six of us in a revolving restaurant at the top of the world staring into the mist—only imagining what may be beyond
So I left Schilthorn in the mist—and that was my experience of it—a mist that surrounded it and enveloped it—a mist that appeared to go forever
And is this not the lives we live—for we were born in the mist—and could only imagine what is beyond
In the mist of ignorance of the Magnificence of this World
In the mist of ignorance of the Magnificence of our Lives
In the mist of ignorance of the Magnificence of Who We Are
That day in Switzerland I left the mountain in the mist—and took that memory with me
Years later I saw a picture of the view from Schilthorn—it took my breath away—there were mountain tops stretching forever in the distance in all directions—stunning beyond imagining

As the mist veiling our lives
—at times we may have craved to see what was beyond
—and yet through the pain and trauma in the ignorance of
our Truth, there was a comfort and security in the mist
and an unease to see beyond
For what if the pull to our Truth was not real
—and the reality beyond the mist was more the same
That we could not bear
For the hope of the Light we saw in our Dreams pulled us
forward and gave us the strength to walk the road
And then one day the mist of our world slowly lifts and we
see a World and a Reality and a Truth stunning beyond
our imaginings
And we smile for we know that the Dreams we had in the
mist pulling us forward was—Ourselves Calling us Home.

Possibilities Yet To Become

It is the depth of the night
Finally the human activity after a hot summer's day is subsiding
What hidden reasons in the human psyche drives people to pick up pace
in the heat—in the stifling heat of a summer's day
I sit on the top balcony and stare into the darkness of the night
Only the pinpoints of the lights of man and the lights of the Heavens
pierce its symmetry and the world is hidden in the shadows
How curious we perceive the darkness as empty
And yet—the richness of the night tantalizes all the senses with what is
unseen—with what is and with what is not and with what could be
The alertness of the Mind heightens—relishing in the experience of
entering the worlds of possibilities beyond the obvious and the known
The Mind skips a beat—delighting in the adventure of birthing to the
Awareness of the Conscious mind that which is yet unborn
The tantalising worlds beyond the current understanding and beyond the
grasp of the human mind—yet a babe in the Universe of Knowledge
The as yet mysterious worlds of unknown Truths
—the world of the Void, both full and empty
—and the world of Pure Potential and of Possibilities yet To Become
And as I sit on the balcony and breathe in the cool crisp air and stare into
the inky darkness and swim in the Silence at this most Divine of hours—
I contemplate the exciting journeys yet ahead for Man
—Of questions yet to be unravelled
—Of knowledge yet to be realized
—Of futures yet to discovered
—And Possibilities yet to be Created
In this Grand Quest of knowing ourselves
And this Grand Adventure of experiencing ourselves
In this Most Grand and Glorious Universe that is our Home.

Rest Gently Dearest Soul

Another young life so abruptly ended
A Beautiful Light too fragile for this difficult world
Unable to cope with the density and tragedy that this Life can bring and that this Life can be
They will analyse his actions and non-actions and come up with reasons—maybe something in his past caused this painful life
Maybe
In Truth, at a deep level a sensitive Soul could not deal with the harshness of this reality
And so searches for help and digs deeper into the density
A tragedy for a lost Soul and a tragedy for a Light Soul that did not find freedom
A Soul that did not hear the Song of his own Heart—Beautiful beyond measure
A Soul that became trapped in a tormented mind
The sadness for a Beautiful Heart that never found fulfilment
And now he rests in the Loving arms of the Angels and will find the Peace and Joy that he did not find here in this beautiful but difficult realm
A difficult Life despite all the Love that surrounded him and a sad death
Was he traumatized at the thought of losing his mother?
This not a heartless person but a sensitive Soul experiencing a tragic disconnect between what he believed to be real and what is Truly Real
For in Truth this most Gentle and Loving Soul lost his road back to himself and his Life lost all connection and all meaning

For it is in Connection with our True Selves that we find all we seek—Love and Peace—Hope and Purpose—Joy and Fulfilment

"Rest gently Dearest Soul for you are Home now
Rest in the arms of God—safe and secure and Much Loved
It was but a dream, Dearest One—whether a good dream or a bad dream, nevertheless a dream
You did not fail—you played a tragedy on this stage of Life that is all
So rest easy Dearest, for your suffering within the dream is over and you are Home
And when you are ready you may choose to venture out again on another Grand Adventure."

Shine the Light of Your Sun for All to See

The dawn awakens—thank God!!
The night was long—drifting in and out of realities I thought had long gone
The pain—the sorrow—the disempowerment—the terror yet again of
falling into that abyss of fear from which the exit was so long
Slowly I clawed my way out ever screaming to the Heavens to rescue me
from that hell
"May Day, May Day, May Day"
Familiar sounds many a time beamed out in desperation through the
darkness in the depth of the despair

And yet I now awake and watch the glorious dawn
—the dawn of the day and the dawn of my life
I watch the iridescent Sun as its Brilliance lights up the cool morning sky
and plays hide and seek with the clouds

"It was but a nightmare Little One"

I hear the gentle whisper on the breeze as it caresses my face

"Do not weep, you are in the dawn of your Glorious New Day
A day that will shine long and you will warm many yet in the winter of
their lives
So toss the embers of your nightmares into your Glorious Sun
Give thanks for its Life
And give Gratitude for all that have Loved you through the nightmare to the
dawn and now share in your glory
Breathe deep and stand tall Dear One for the Divine Ones are with you
Sing your Glorious Song and shine the Light of your Sun for all to see
That they may breathe in Life and Hope on their journey to their dawn when
one day they too will awake and shine in the Splendour of their own Light."

The Brushstrokes of a Grand Masterpiece

A glorious morning on a glorious autumn day on a Beautiful World
What have we done to be so Blessed?
A Moment in time that will be forever carried in my memory on my journeys here and beyond—adding to so many glorious memories
Memories I shall treasure of my amazing time on this most Divine of Worlds
A dove coos in the trees above and carries me with it as its sound proclaims its Presence
This most Precious Gift of Time—it is but a mere blink in the eye of God
And yet the Treasure runs deep
For we can experience Infinity
And we can see the colours of the rainbow
And we can hear the Divine sounds of the myriad forms of Life that travel with us
And we can touch Reality and taste it and revel in it
And philosophize about it
And have opinions about our view of the world and what it all means
As we express our own uniqueness and share our Wisdom as we know it with all that share this Precious World
And through it all, experience what evolves from our individual and collective Wisdom
The Joy of Life—the Joy of pure Creation

To start with the first word of a poem or a story
—or the first idea of a new thought
—or the first brushstroke on a canvas
—or the first hit of a ball
—or the first step of whatever the Heart chooses
and watch the magic as the masterpiece evolves before our eyes
For a Masterpiece It Is and It Must Be
—for we and this Beautiful World and this Beautiful Universe that we share are the brushstrokes of a Grand Masterpiece from the Grandest Master of All
And we carry the Essence of that Master and that Mastery
And so as we go about our days in whatever we do—to appreciate this most Precious Life—where we can Be the Creators of our own Masterpiece
And so add to the Brushstrokes of a Far Grander Picture
What a Joy and what a Privilege this Life is.

The Dance of Light with Density

The beautiful night intoxicates the senses
Delicious beyond the most delicious delight of the taste buds
The body tastes the night with all the senses
It stimulates all that is human and all that is Divine
With Being beyond the understanding of human experience
I do not have the words to describe the Beauty of the Moment
—to describe the Power of the Moment or
—to describe my Connection with the Moment
It is beyond words—it is beyond feelings—and it is beyond experience
It is Connection at a fundamental level of Truth
A merging of my Truth with the Truth that is around me
And in that merging I experience the Truth of that which is around me as both separate to me and both as Me
Separation and Unity—all at the one time—all in the one Moment—all in the same experience
How exquisite
Human and Divine experiencing at the same time—in the same breath—in the same Moment

"Do you understand Dearest Ones what a Gift this is?
Do you understand Dearest Ones what a Gift Human Life is?
To experience both Separation and Oneness at once
To experience your Humanness and your Divinity at the same time

And through the experience
—Divinity experiences what it is to be Human, through its
Truth of its Humanity
—and the Human experiences what it is to be Divine, through
its Truth of its Divinity
The Dance across time and space
The Dance of God with Man
The Dance of Truth with Matter
The Dance of Light with Density
You are much Blessed my Dearest Ones
You are much Loved and you are much Treasured
Value what you have been honoured with My Loved Ones
For it is Truly a Gift of the Divine."

The Dance of the Divine

The days are long
Betrayal and pain in the world of man
All is not what it seems—all is illusion
All are shadows playing out a game that has no meaning unto itself
The Truth of the world reversed—the illusion is complete

"Do not be fooled Dearest Ones
Do not place meaning where it does not belong—for it will dive you into despair
Do not try and find Love amongst the shadows—for in that search you will be disillusioned
—and thinking that you have failed, intensify the search and become more and more desperate as it eludes you
—and you sink deeper and deeper into the illusion
Stop your search Dearest Ones
Be still
Breathe deep and breathe easy
Feel the Pulse of Life
Look at the Wondrous Creation around you and through you and within you
Feel the breeze on your face and give thanks for the Life you experience
Go Dance with the wind and delight in the ripples you create on the water and laugh with it as it rustles through the trees
Share in Life Dearest Ones and Enjoy the beautiful world you are a part of

*Open your eyes and see that it is all born of Love
All of Creation is a 'Love' Child
So rest easy My Beloved Ones—breathe deep
You do not need to seek Love for it has never left you—it could not
For you are born of Divine Love
And the fabric of your Being is sculptured from Divine Love
And your very Essence beats to the pulse of Divine Love—
As does all Creation
So know Your Truth My Dearest Ones
And as you Dance your Dance with Creation
Know that it too Dances the Dance of Love with You
Love touching Love—Lovemaking at its most profound—
The Dance of the Divine."*

The Gift of True Life

Another glorious day is ending on Planet Earth
I sit on my Beloved Rocks overlooking my Beloved Ocean
feeling the breeze on my body
And surrounded by the magnificent fiery iridescent streaks
of the Sunset across the Heavens
My eyes are drawn up to a Reality beyond the mundane
trivia of our small lives
I wonder back to today
In how many moments—of oh so many moments today—
was I Truly Alive?
In how many moments—of oh so many moments today—
did I Truly Delight and give Gratitude for being here on this
Jewel of a gift, Planet Earth?
In how many moments—of oh so many moments today—
was I Truly Present?
In how many moments—of oh so many moments today—
did I Truly know who I Am?
In how many moments—of oh so many moments today—
did I Truly Share the gift of who I Am with the world?
And my answer comes—with sadness at the realization—
Oh so few—so very few
Even one Divine Moment missed in the unconscious dream
state—as the seconds of our short life drift away—is a travesty

"Imagine being alive in even one full Moment
—in which you are Truly Alive
—in which you live to the Truth that You Are

*—in which you live to the Truth of your Connection to Life
and all living things
—in which you Truly feel the Heart that beats in your chest
and the Heart that beats in creation—and Know they are One?
This Dearest Ones is the True Treasure of Life
There is not enough gold on your beautiful planet to the
power of Infinity that could pay for such a Gift
The Gift of True Life
When man in flesh looks to the Heavens and says—
'Yes I Am All that I Am and its sweetness is Divine'
Imagine even one day filled with Infinite Moments of Being
Truly Alive
Do you begin to understand Dearest Ones the enormity of
this Gift?
And can you imagine a lifetime filled with such Moments?
Your Truth will change the face of the Earth forever and
your Song will be heard throughout the Heavens
Glory to you Dearest Ones
This world awaits you."*

The Journey Of The Soul

My days are long
There is much clutter in my world
Letters to write, negotiations to conduct, people to meet
The clutter of the mundane world
And yet I yearn to sit on my Beloved Rocks overlooking my Beloved Ocean
And Fly to the horizon and melt with the Sunset
And Dance with the cool breeze that caresses my face
How do I reconcile these worlds?
One the world of Man and the construct of his mind
The other—the world of my Truth where my Spirit and my Soul and my Being fly free
One a world caged by the tight boundaries of the limitations of the consciousness of Matter and of the consciousness of Man
The other—the Boundless World of my Infinite Truth where All exists—and reality and non-reality are both real in the Infinite Potential of what is possible
I am at that sweet junction where my Consciousness holds both but I have not yet integrated them—for I prefer to fly free on the wind or go play with the Dolphins or make love to the night than sit in a closed room doing some mundane task in the world of Man
How do I reconcile these worlds?
I do not know at this stage—but is this not the sweetness of the journey through the world of Matter?
I do know—that I Will reach that Integration when the mundane too will become Divine

And I will fly free on the wind and play with the Dolphins and make love to the night regardless of what I am doing in the world of Man
And in that Glorious Moment—the mundane will dissolve back into the Divine from whence it came
From Love back to Love
From Beauty back to Beauty
From The Divine back to the Divine
The Journey of the Soul
The Journey Home
And what a Grand Journey it is.

The Moment Contains the All

The Delight of the Moment

"Why do you will more Dear Ones?
Do you not see that the Moment contains the All?
How can you will more than the All?
The lack is not in the Moment but in your
realization of the Moment
Gain the realization and you will understand that
the Universe lies at your feet
And then your Life will be fulfilled
For you have All—in every breath, in every blink,
in every Moment, of every day of your Life here on
this Beautiful World and beyond."

True Choice

How do I jump this chasm of distraught?
How do I manage this chasm of discomfort?
How do I make sense of this senseless disempowerment?
How do I let go of this agony within my Being?
How do I get back to Joy—where I fly free with the wind and play with the clouds and melt at the sunset and Dance with the waves?

"Do you not see Dearest Ones it is pure Choice—for All exists in the Moment
Both Heaven and Hell exist Now and in every Moment
They must in the glorious world of duality
Otherwise Life as you know it could not exist
Your journey however is not about going from no choice to choice
It is not about going to university and achieving a degree in advanced choice making
—so you can finally live your Life with choice
But to realize that from the Moment that you came into existence you have always had choice—in every breath—in every Moment of your Life
Only Dearest Ones you did not know it
So the journey has never been one of learning how to make choices—
but to realize that choices—all choices—are your birthright and have always been so
Simple really—your journey is to reach the realization that you have choice—
True Choice—and know it—your choice!!
Understand though Dearest Ones that True Choice is not within the world of duality
—deciding between left and right, between night and day, between light and dark, between suffering and non-suffering

For in the world of duality choosing one of these will also bring its opposite
Choice within the world of duality is a parameter of the game
Enjoy the game—enjoy the duality
For within it you can experience the grand wonders of the world you live in
Within it you can touch the flowers, feel the breeze, see the glories around you and taste the nectar of Life—you can breathe it in till All Your Being tingles with the Joy of Life

True Choice is the choice to choose your Truth—the Truth that you Are— above the Game—beyond the world of duality
Realize Dearest Ones that your Truth is far Grander than the beautiful realm of duality
Choose your Truth—and you will bring Heaven to Earth
You will anchor the Truth that You Are in the world of duality
Then my Dearest Ones watch what happens
You become the Creator of the game—your game
And your Choices are now Infinite
From the Infinite back to the Infinite with Conscious Choice
What an extraordinary Life you Live Dearest Ones
You are a Joy to behold
Enjoy."

Truth of My Being

I awake from a troubled sleep
I go outside to shift the heaviness around my Being
It is the depth of the night and the world sleeps
The cool crisp air and vivid sharpness of the light of the night at this most Divine time greets me
The earth is cool and damp after the previous night of heavy rain
—the Rain, the Rain, the Glorious Rain
The only sounds to be heard are the roar of the Ocean waves in the distance as they crash to the shore and the soft rustle of the trees as they sway with the gentle breeze
There are no sounds from the human world
It is as if it does not exist at this most Divine of hours deep into the night
The only tell-tale signs are the linear silhouettes of man's creation and the sharp pinpoints of street lights in the distance
The Silence is delicious
My Heart lifts as I Merge with the stunning Reality around me
I look up to the Stars and skip a beat in the awesome beauty of the canopy of lights stretching forever into the depths of the night sky
The fluffy white clouds luminesce against the darkness of space
My Heart lifts and My Soul sings as I stare at the Stars and as I expand into the Truth of My Home on this Magnificent world and in this Magnificent universe
The troubled mind and the troubled heart—that was all-consuming a mere few moments ago—has taken on its true insignificance in the awesome grandeur of The Truth of My Being and the Totality of Who I Am

The self-imposed shackles of the self-imposed limitation of the
disempowerment of my Truth to my thoughts and actions of
my day-to-day human existence
—fades to its true perspective in the expanding awareness of Truth—
Truth of my Heart—Truth of my Soul—And Truth of my Being
—on the Infinite journey of the Divine through created reality
My Heart sings in Joy and Gratitude and Wonder for the realization of
Truth of this wondrous Life on this most Divine of worlds in this most
extraordinary Universe that is our Home
My eyes are drawn to the horizon by a brilliant light hanging low in the
night sky
Ah! it is Venus, a jewel in the night sky, greeting this Beautiful World
and keeping vigil at this most Divine of hours
I am drawn back to the delicious cool crispness in the air and the Silence
The wind has died down and the waves are still
And the Silence is the only sound to be heard
I smile as I sink into it as it wraps me in its Presence
The Silence, the Divine Silence runs deep
And in the depth of the Silence I hear the Hum
Is it the Hum of Mother Earth breathing?
Is it the Hum of the Universe?
Perhaps it is the Hum of Life itself
And then the rain gently starts to fall
I smile and I laugh as I pick up my things and run onto the balcony
What a Precious and Extraordinary Life we Live.

"Wake Up, Wake Up My Beautiful Children"

The days are long—much to do in the chaos of man's world
All seems so distant as the days are filled with meaningless
clutter—actions that serve no purpose in the grand scheme
of the Journey of our Lives
Minutiae—staring at the dust particles on the floor of a
mansion of gold and jewels and beauty beyond comprehension
As we sit and focus our attention on removing a smudge of
dirt in Paradise
So insignificant—such a waste of our Precious Life Force
Such a dumbing down of the Magnificence of our Being and
the Awesomeness of our Journey
For we have travelled the Universe and played hide and seek
with the Stars
We have ridden the moonbeams and surfed the Oceans
We have watched Stars explode and Stars reborn
And we sit in the corner of Paradise
—lost to the Magnificence of our Truth—scrubbing at a
smudge as if it was everything
How sad
The memory of our Truth quashed and the tragedy of the
Moment

*"Wake up, wake up My Beautiful Children—for you are the
Children of God
Arise from the pits of ignorance and remember Who You Are
For the Universe is your Home and You sit at the table of the
Divine
Come my Beautiful Ones Come—We Await You."*

What a Grand Journey We Travel

What a Grand Journey We Travel
Into the depths of the density we threw ourselves with excitement
And hit the heaviness, amnesia, pain and ignorance
Lost in the annals of time and space—lost in the depths of we know not where
Far away from all we know To Be True
Far away from all we know To Be Real
Slowly we adjust to living in the heaviness—living in the trauma of a forgotten reality
The pain of our existence—the pain of our loss—the pain of a difficult life and unfamiliar heaviness
And slowly we adjust to the trauma of a life without memory
And yet—at some level something stirs within our Being—
at some level we still know—at some level we still remember
—Remember Our Heritage
—Remember Our Life
—Remember Our Truth
And slowly through the eons the veil lifts and our memory returns of Our True Home
And with each passing Moment our excitement grows at our return journey Home
And with each passing Moment we relax into our existence for we know we are going Home
We relax and we start to appreciate the Wonderful World we are living in

The world we thought was our jailer from our Truth
—in Truth nurtured us and cared for us in our despair
We could not see its Beauty, or feel its Love, or feel its
Connection through the pain and despair of our loss
And as we prepare to go Home—we grow in our Love and
appreciation of the Love of this Beautiful Jewel of a World that
has become Our Home away from Home
And so the journey ends where the journey began
And yet in the interlude we are changed forever
For we have seen the hues of the rainbow after the rain
We have felt the wind caress our body
We have climbed the mountains and surfed the waves
We have roared with laughter over a silly joke with a friend
We have felt the pulse of Life around us and joined in its
endless cycles of birth and death
We have been conqueror and conquered
We have felt hate and anger, Love and Joy
We have felt lonely, crushed, misunderstood and adored and
exalted
We have felt pain and ecstasy
And through it all we have gained Understanding, Humility
and Wisdom
And through it all we have lived and have been part of this
wonderful thing we call Life

Cont ...

Then as we reach the end of our journey—the Greatest Gift of All opens to us and we smile to the Heavens and bow as we start to Dance
The Dance between God and His Children
The Dance between Man and the Divine
The Dance between Heaven and Earth
And the Laughter can be heard and the Delight felt throughout Creation and the Heavens
And the Joy within merges to the Joy without
The circle is complete
What a Grand Journey this has been
Wouldn't have changed it for anything.

Who and What will You BE
On the Blank Canvass of Your Day?

Another day
So much to do!!—so little time!!
The day is filled with things to do and the stress of not getting them done
Too many, too many, too many things to do!!
I have the list—forget the list!!—I'm never going to get them all done today in any case
What was it I was doing?—can't remember—oh well forget it!!—I'll do something else
And so we run from one act of doing to another act of doing—a slave by any name

"My Dearest Ones your days will go by whether in slavery or Freedom—the difference can be but a blink away
For it is not your doing that determines your Freedom—it is your Being
And once you are Free—your doing also becomes liberated as it takes on its Truth as the Dance of Who You Are
And so My Dearest Ones, did you wake today and give Gratitude for another Precious Day?
Did you watch the sun rise and hear the birds sing and hear the wind as it rustles through the trees?
Did you Create your day and infuse it with Love and Gratitude and Joy and Laughter and Fun?
Did you grasp the Grand Opportunity of another Glorious Day on your world to Create the day as your own?
So My Dearest Ones who and what will you BE on the Blank Canvas of Your Day on your Beautiful Blue-Green Jewel of a Home?"

You Are The Purpose

The night shines brightly tonight
A Gift from the Divine
Another day in glorious manifested reality

"Have you ever wondered about the possibility of your existence?
An infinitesimal probability—and so your life is improbable and yet here you are!!
Looking through eyes and seeing the colours of the rainbow, hearing the sounds of life, tasting the sweet nectar of reality and feeling the pulse of this extraordinary existence that you are privileged to experience—from an improbable possibility!!
Is this not something to Celebrate Dearest Ones?
Does this not fire your Heart and fire your Soul with the Extraordinary Life you live?

So why my Dearest and Precious Ones do you take it all for granted?
Why do look for a purpose outside of yourself?
For your existence at all is one of the Grandest achievements of Reality
Do you not understand how Precious your Life is?
Yet in your ignorance you give it little value
And so search for value beyond you and purpose beyond your existence
And so search for reasons that exist outside of Truth

You are in such a hurry to 'Go Home'
Dearest you are Home—Dearest You Are home—it could not be otherwise
Your precious experience in the glorious reality you live in is not outside of who you are—it cannot be—you could not and would not exist

Your experience is the Divine Dance of who You Are
—flowing and moving and experiencing
—and relishing in the experience of Self
—and all that you are in Truth
—and all that you are Creating
—and all that you are Becoming
—and all that you are Birthing within and through this extraordinary reality
For the Wonder of All—for the Wonder of You
So My Precious Ones do not be so eager to Go Home
You Are Home—you have never left it!!
You are The Treasure
You are The Gift
You are The Purpose
So Enjoy, my Beautiful Ones, Enjoy!!
You are much Loved and you are much Treasured."

PART FIVE

The Driver is Love

The Driver is Love

I sit on the top balcony of my home on a divine morning, cool and wet after a long dry summer
I reflect back to yesterday—it was a day of family and friends, food and celebration
The excuse was my birthday—however the reason was the gathering of family and friends

It was a poignant day
I held the celebration at my home
—my beautiful home that my parents built oh so long ago
It was a day that repeated itself a generation on
My parents held a similar celebration in the same backyard for my 21st birthday all those years ago
My uncles and aunties were all there—as were the paesani, their friends of their generation
I and my brother and cousins were the children
We took a group photo yesterday from the balcony into the courtyard, as we did all those years ago—only time has moved on and the faces are different

My parents and uncles and aunties are dead
And yet they live on
I felt their Presence yesterday as they celebrated with us on a day of celebration
Celebration of the love and friendship that is shared between us
Celebration of the Joy of Life
And Celebration of the flow of humanity from one generation to the next

An individual Life is short—oh so short!!
It was but yesterday that it was my 21st birthday—
and there are moments I blink and as I open my eyes I expect to see my parents and aunties and uncles
And then realize they are not with us—here on this plane of reality
But they are with us
And that is the True Celebration!!
For we never stand alone
And what appears to be a short isolated life is far from the Truth

For we are a part of a far Grander Picture
We stand on the shoulders of those that came before us
And we all support those that come after us
As humanity moves forward from humble beginnings oh so long ago
An expansion from ignorance to greater and greater levels of awareness and all that embraces
Of the Power and the Privilege and Magnificence and True Significance of this Extraordinary Journey of Life we share together across generations and across time and space
Of the Privilege to Experience and to Strive and to Share and to Create and to Make a Difference for the Better
—for ourselves and our loved ones and our world and beyond

Cont …

And the Driver is Love
In All its forms, Divine and human and at All levels
Love of life—Love of experiencing—Love of creating—Love of family—
Love of people—Love of sharing—and Love of caring
And out of that Love we Spiral Upwards to greater levels of Awareness
And greater levels of Wisdom
And greater levels of Intelligence
And greater levels of Understanding
And greater levels of Experience
And greater levels of Connection
And greater levels of Creation
And greater and greater levels of Love and Joy

And so the journey spirals onwards and upwards
And what a Grand Journey it is
Wouldn't miss it for anything.

www.ingramcontent.com/pod-product-compliance
Lightning Source LLC
Chambersburg PA
CBHW061136010526
44107CB00068B/2965